THE BLENHEIM ROLL, 1704.

THE BLENHEIM ROLL,

1704.

EDITED AND ANNOTATED BY

CHARLES DALTON, F.R.G.S.,

Member of the Scottish History Society; Honorary Member of the Royal
United Service Institution, and Royal Artillery Institution.

*Editor of the "Waterloo Roll Call," "English Army Lists and Commission
Registers, 1661-1714," &c., &c.*

The Naval & Military Press Ltd

In reprinting in facsimile from the original, any imperfections are inevitably reproduced and the quality may fall short of modern type and cartographic standards.

DEDICATED TO

ISABELLA DALTON DALTON,

BY

HER HUSBAND.

CONTENTS.

	PAGE
INTRODUCTION	ix
Staff	1–7
Train of Artillery	8–11
Hospital	12
Lieut.-General Lumley's Regt. of Horse	13–15
Major-General Wood's Regt. of Horse	16–17
Brigadier-General Cadogan's Regt. of Horse	18–19
Lieut.-General Wyndham's Regt. of Horse	20–21
The Duke of Schomberg's Regt. of Horse	22–23
Lord John Hay's Regt. of Dragoons	24–26
Major-General Ross's Regt. of Dragoons	27–28
First Regt. of Foot Guards (1st Batt.)	29–32
First Batt. Royal Regt. of Foot	33–35
Second Batt. Royal Regt. of Foot	36–38
General Churchill's Regt. of Foot	39–41
Brigadier-General Webb's Regt. of Foot	42–44
Lord North and Grey's Regt. of Foot	45–47
Brigadier-General Howe's Regt. of Foot	48–50
The Earl of Derby's Regt. of Foot	51–53
Brigadier-General Hamilton's Regt. of Foot	54–56
Brigadier-General Row's Regt. of Fusiliers	57–59
Lieut.-General Ingoldsby's Regt. of Fusiliers	60–62
The Duke of Marlborough's Regt. of Foot	63–65
Brigadier-General Ferguson's Regt. of Foot	66–68
Brigadier-General Meredyth's Regt. of Foot	69–71
List of the widows or children of the slain officers of the Regiments afore-mentioned	72
Abstract of the distribution of the Prize Money	73
Index	75–82

INTRODUCTION.

THE MS. known as the "Blenheim Bounty Roll" is preserved at the Public Record Office (*Treasury Papers*, Vol. XCIII., No. 79). It was prepared under the direction of the Duke of Marlborough and the General Officers who served under him in Germany during the memorable campaign of 1704. The aforesaid military board had to determine the scale of blood-money due to all the British officers and soldiers, in the Queen's pay, who had shared in the victories of Schellenberg (2 July), and Blenheim (13 August), which thereby entitled them to participate in the bounty money Queen Anne bestowed upon her victorious troops in March 1705. The Royal bounty included grants to the widows of the officers (p. 72) and soldiers killed during the campaign in question, or who died from their wounds prior to the preparation of the bounty lists. From the following pages it will be seen that Marlborough, as Captain-General of the Army, received £600 (which sum he voluntarily resigned in order to increase the bounty fund); while the sur awarded to privates and drummers (the Foot Guards excepted) was £1 per man. Wounded officers and men received double the amount granted to those who escaped unhurt; and all staff officers whose regiments took part in the campaign were respectively entitled to two shares.

Unique and interesting as the MS. Bounty Roll undoubtedly is, it may be said to require a key. In the first place many of the officers' names given in the said Roll are unrecognisable from mis-spelling, and a large proportion of the surnames are devoid of their christian appellations. Orthography was of no account in Marlborough's time. The Duke himself was an erratic speller, and one at least of his best generals found it a laborious task to put pen to paper. The following certificate written and signed by Colonel (afterwards Lieut.-General) Richard Ingoldsby, in 1692, is still extant:*

"I dow att the request of Mrs. Eliz. Danvers serthyfi that Capt. Mick Miller was kiltt att the newry onder my command the 24 of November 1689 as witness my hand this 14 of Jully 1692. RICH. INGOLDESBY."

The Editor has carefully revised all the surnames in the following pages and has added, between square brackets, the Christian names of officers whenever ascertainable from reliable sources. The MS. Bounty Roll cannot be said to be a complete list of officers who served at Schellenberg and Blenheim. A goodly number of officers who were killed, or died from their wounds, at the before named battles are omitted altogether from the Roll because they left no widows or children to claim the bounty to which they were entitled. To remedy this obvious defect the Editor has also added, between brackets, such officers who were killed at Schellenberg and Blenheim, or who died from their wounds. It may be mentioned that the casualties at Blenheim are taken from a *List of the Officers killed and dead of the wounds they received at the Battle of Blenheim*, which MS. was prepared for the Duke of Marlborough after the battle, and is now at the Public Record Office (*Auxiliary Expeditions*, 1704). The casualties at Schellenberg are specially referred to by the Editor in his annotations, and are for the most part given on the authority of the official returns printed in Lediard's *Life of Marlborough*. It must be remembered that the same regiments which fought at Schellenberg took part in the battle of Blenheim, and that the completeness of the latter victory was due, to some extent, to the severe defeat

---

* *Treasury Papers*, Vol. xix., No. 16, Public Record Office.

of the French and Bavarians in the former sanguinary contest.

Of course some regiments, the Royal Scots Dragoons, for instance, were more actively engaged in one battle than in the other, while some battalions, notably the 1st Foot Guards, bore the brunt of the fighting in both engagements. At the storming of the heights of the Schellenberg (the hill of the tinkling bell) the 1st Foot Guards had the honour to supply the forlorn hope which preceded the picked body of infantry selected to lead the assault on the enemy's entrenchments. The intrepid Lord Mordaunt, son and heir of the renowned Earl of Peterborough, commanded the forlorn hope on this memorable occasion, and it is on record that out of a total of fifty grenadiers only ten, besides himself, came out of action. Twice were the body of stormers and their supports driven back by the enemy, who were very strongly entrenched. The carnage on both sides was fearful.* For the third time the trenches were assaulted and the defenders driven back slowly but steadily. At this crisis in the battle, Lord John Hay dismounted the Royal Scots Dragoons, who were formed as infantry, and joined the assailants. The trenches carried, the Scots Dragoons remounted and charged with the body of cavalry which Marlborough now hurled against the Bavarian and French troops, who were completely routed and chased to the banks of the Danube, where many of them were drowned in their attempt to escape. Without going into dull statistics it may be said that the British and their Allies lost very heavily at Schellenberg. Marlborough did not exaggerate when he described the aforesaid action as "the warmest that has been known for many years."

---

* In 1705, a traveller (M. de Blainville), visiting the scene of conflict, remarked a vast quantity of skulls and bones in the fosses of the works, and amidst a heap of old rags an English Grenadier's cap, on a fragment of which the Queen's motto, "Semper Eadem," was still legible. *Naval and Military Gazette,* 19 October, 1850.

The story of Blenheim has been written over and over again, and the subject is not yet exhausted. Addison's muse immortalised the campaign of 1704, and his simile of "the angel" was not thought over-drawn when his poem first appeared in print. His poetic effusion certainly helped him up several rungs on the ladder of fame. Colonel Blackader has left us a descriptive narration in prose of the great victory from a stern Scottish soldier's point of view. Creasy has placed Blenheim among the fifteen decisive battles of the world.* The Abbé Dutems's *Histoire de Jean Churchill, Duc de Marlborough* (Paris, 1808) was compiled by direction of Napoleon. The various lives of Prince Eugène of Savoy do adequate justice to the leading part played by Marlborough at Blenheim. Within the last few months the author of *Fights for the Flag* has given us a thrilling word-sketch— *Marlborough at Blenheim* (*Cornhill Magazine*, August, 1898). Green, the historian, has ably upheld the importance of Marlborough's greatest victory.† The Rev. Francis Hare's journal of the campaign of 1704 (printed in the *Marlborough Dispatches*) gives a truthful and succinct account by a forward eye-witness of the glorious actions in Germany. Colonel John Ivoy, who served with the Allied Army at Blenheim, has left a well-executed plan of the field of battle, which has been lately reproduced for a military journal (*R.U.S. Institution Journal* for September, 1898.) Brigadier-General Richard Kane, who participated in Marlborough's brilliant victories, left a posthumous work, entitled, *Narrative of Campaigns in*

---

* "Had it not been for Blenheim," wrote Sir Edward Creasy, "all Europe might at this day suffer under the effect of French conquests, resembling those of Alexander in extent, and those of the Romans in durability."

† "The loss of France," wrote Green, "could not be measured by men or fortresses. A hundred victories since Rocroi had taught the world to regard the French army as invincible, when Blenheim, and the surrender of the flower of the French soldiery, broke the spell." *History of the English People.*

the reigns of William III. and Queen Anne (published in 1745). Lediard's *Life of Marlborough* (3 volumes) was a standard work in the last century, and is still a reliable account of the great Duke's military actions. Sergeant Millner's *Journal* gives a non-commissioned officer's unvarnished relation of the battles and sieges in which he took part (published in 1733). Oldmixon, the historian, and Prior celebrated Blenheim in verse. Captain Robert Parker of the Royal Irish Regiment of Foot, who fought at Blenheim, has also left a very readable story of Marlborough's wars (published in 1746). Southey's versatile genius produced a poem on the battle of Blenheim a hundred years ago. The cynical Byron hailed with delight Archdeacon Coxe's painstaking and conscientious work:—

> "The world was growing 'dim' to the great Marlbro's skill
>   in giving knocks,
> Until his late life by Archdeacon Coxe"——

Alison, the historian, portrayed Marlborough's military life, and the facile pen of one who is a master in the art of war, and can clothe the bare bones of strategy with the true spirit of warfare, is now engaged on the history of Marlborough's meteoric career.

But what of Marlborough's companions in arms—the officers who taught, drilled, and led the British squadrons and battalions which forced the stubborn foe to yield at Schellenberg and Blenheim. Are the waters of Lethe to engulf the names of those brave men who assisted in building up the British Empire by gaining victories which were only won by discipline, pluck, endurance, lives sacrificed, wounds received, limbs lost, health impaired? Up to the present time no one has recorded, collectively, the names of the Blenheim heroes or cared to trace their anterior or subsequent careers. Many of the officers in question had served nearly a score of years in the British army, and had earned fame and distinction on several hard-fought battle-fields. There were grey-haired subalterns at Blenheim who had received commissions from the ranks for former acts of gallantry.* As drill-instructors these veterans were invaluable, and their presence did much to steady the ranks at Blenheim, Ramillies, Oudenarde, and Malplaquet. A tablet here, a memoir there, and a rough MS. list of the recipients of Queen Anne's bounty after Blenheim, may be said to be all that is left to remind us of the British officers composing the army which was mainly instrumental in checkmating Louis XIV. in his attempt to establish a sort of universal empire. It is true that the changes have been rung on Marlborough, and most deservedly too; but is the leader of an army the only person to be remembered—the only one to be thanked? It is also true that Oldmixon, in his *History of Queen Anne*, mentions a few of the leading Blenheim officers "whose names ought to live with honour as long as history can preserve them;" but this handful of generals, some of whom fought on the side of our allies, is surely very inadequate. Feeling this very strongly, the Editor makes no apology or excuse for publishing the *Blenheim Roll*. He is well aware that military records of the far past "do not appeal to the public taste" except when these same records are interwoven with fiction. At the present time the Dutch military authorities are instituting a diligent search for records bearing on the history of their army in the past; but it will be very long before the British War Office, or any eclectic society, attempt to bring to light the rich stores of military MSS. hidden in our national archives. "We have no hesitation in asserting," says the *Athenæum* of 23 May 1896, "that a systematic description and collation of the original materials that exist for the military history of this country, or, in other words, for the making of the empire, is a work that nearly concerns our national honour."

The same lack of interest shown in England for old

---

* A notable instance was Robert Parker of the Royal Irish Regt. of Foot, who was given a Commission as Ensign in said corps for his gallantry at the siege of Namur. *See* p. 55, note 15.

military records formerly extended to the trophies won by our army on celebrated battle-fields. Where are the thirty-four standards and eighty-three colours captured at Blenheim which fell to Marlborough's share of the spoils, and which he brought to London in December 1704? History records that these same trophies were carried in military procession on 3 January 1705, from the Tower to Westminster Hall through the City, and thence by way of the Strand, Pall Mall, and St. James's Park, where Queen Anne viewed the *cortége* from Lord Fitzharding's house. The plaudits of the populace on the line of route, and the booming of cannon, celebrated the glorious triumph of British arms. After being exhibited in Westminster Hall, the Blenheim standards and colours * found a final resting place in St. Paul's Cathedral. On the 2nd November 1835, the Reverend Sydney Smith (the Canon), writing to General Sir Herbert Taylor on the subject of the Blenheim trophies, said *not a rag, not a staff remained!* It is a fact worth remembering that the Douglas banner † carried at the battle of "Chevy Chase" (Otterburn) in 1388, is still in existence and in wonderful preservation. Time's destroying hand is not, therefore, wholly answerable for the total destruction of the Blenheim colours, but the wilful and culpable negligence of the guardians of these interesting relics.

CHARLES DALTON.

---

* An exact account of the Blenheim standards and colours was taken in writing, in December 1704, by order of the Rt. Hon. Robert Harley, Secretary of State, whilst the said trophies were lying in the Tower of London. This MS. account, which gives all the mottoes, devices, and heraldic descriptions, was found by the Editor of the Blenheim Roll at the Public Record Office (*Ordnance Warrants*, Vol XLIX., pp. 386 *et seq.*), and edited by him, with explanatory notes, for the *Journal of the R.U.S. Institution* for September 1898.

† This ancient relic is preserved at Cavers House, Co. Roxburgh, and is thirteen feet long. See *The Annals of a Border Club*, by George Tancred, late Captain Scots Greys, pp. 114-117.

ABBREVIATIONS.

Adjt. = Adjutant.
Bd. = Buried.
Brigdr.-Gen. = Brigadier-General.
Bt. = Brevet (when given before military titles).
Cy. = Company.
Comn. = Commission.
Capt.-Lt. = Captain-Lieutenant (*id est,* the officer commanding the Colonel's Troop or Company).
Cor. = Cornet.
C.-in-C. = Commander-in-Chief.
D. = Died.
Dns. = Dragoons.
Ens. = Ensign.
Ft.-Gds. = Foot Guards.
Gov. = Governor.
Grendr. = Grenadier.
H. Gds. = Horse Guards.
Indep. Cy. = Independent Company.
K. after an officer's name = Killed.
Lt. = Lieutenant.
Maj. = Major.
Ml. = Marshal.
Md. = Married.
M. I. = Monumental Inscription.
Prov. = Province.
Qr.-Mr. = Quarter-master.
Regtal. = Regimental.
Retd. = Retired.
Tp. = Troop.
W. after an officer's name = Wounded.
Wt. = Warrant.

THE BLENHEIM ROLL.

STAFF.

	£	s.	d.	
CAPTAIN-GENERAL.				
The Duke of Marlborough [1]	600	0	0	Bounty.
GENERAL OF THE FOOT.				
Charles Churchill [2]	360	0	0	,,
LIEUTS.-GENERAL.				
John, Lord Cutts [3]	240	0	0	,,
Henry Lumley [4]	240	0	0	,,
[George] Earl of Orkney [5]	240	0	0	,,
Richard Ingoldsby [6]	240	0	0	,,
MAJORS-GENERAL.				
Cornelius Wood, [7] W.	120	0	0	,,
Henry Withers [8]	120	0	0	,,
Charles Ross [9]	120	0	0	,,
BRIGADIERS-GENERAL.				
Frederick Hamilton [10]	90	0	0	,,
John [Richmond] Webb [11]	90	0	0	,,
James Ferguson [12]	90	0	0	,,
[Archibald Row, [13] K.]				
William Cadogan [14]	90	0	0	,,
Thomas Meredyth, [15] W.	90	0	0	,,
Francis Palmes [16]	90	0	0	,,
Lord John Hay [17]	90	0	0	,,
ADJUTANT-GENERAL.				
Thomas Meredyth [15]	60	0	0	,,
QUARTER-MASTER-GENERAL.				
William Cadogan [14]	60	0	0	,,
DEPUTY-QUARTER-MASTER-GENERAL.				
Captain Alexander Spottiswood, W. [18]	15	0	0	,,
SECRETARY TO THE CAPTAIN-GENERAL.				
Adam Cardonnel [19]	30	0	0	,,
CHAPLAIN TO THE CAPTAIN-GENERAL.				
[Francis] Hare [20]	20	0	0	,,
PHYSICIAN TO THE CAPTAIN-GENERAL.				
[Dr. Thos. Lawrence [21]]	30	0	0	,,

SURGEON TO THE CAPTAIN-GENERAL.

	£	s.	d.	
[Thos. Gardiner [22]]	30	0	0	Bounty.

DEPUTY JUDGE-ADVOCATE.

Henry Watkins [23]	30	0	0	,,

WAGGON-MASTER-GENERAL.

Colonel [Giles] Spicer [24]	21	7	6	,,

PROVOST-MARSHAL-GENERAL.

Captain [James?] Fury and his two men [25]	36	0	0	,,

AIDES-DE-CAMP TO THE GENERAL OFFICERS.

Lieut.-Colonel [James] Bringfield [26]	30	0	0	,,
,, ,, [Henry] Durell [27]	,,	,,		
,, ,, [Thomas] Panton [28]	,,	,,		
[Lord Tunbridge [29]]	,,	,,		
[Colonel Daniel Parke [30]]	,,	,,		
[Lieut.] Colonel Charles Churchill [31]	,,	,,		
[Lieut.] Colonel [William] Lloyd [32]	,,	,,		
Captain ——— Pitt [33]	,,	,,		
,, [Henry] Disney [34]	,,	,,		
,, [George] Watkins [35]	,,	,,		
,, [Jas.] Eyton [36]	,,	,,		
,, [Francis?] Scawen [37]	,,	,,		
,, [James] Abercrombie [38]	,,	,,		
,, [Matthew] Pennefather [39]	,,	,,		
,, [Isaac] Jevereau,[40] W.	,,	,,		
,, [Anthony] Pujolas [41]	,,	,,		
Lieutenant [Robert?] Wilson [42]	,,	,,		
,, [Peter?] Law [43]	,,	,,		
Cornet [George] Stephenson,[44] W.	,,	,,		
,, [Edward] Hamilton,[45] W.	,,	,,		
[,, Lewis Oglethorpe,[46] K.]	,,	,,		

MAJORS OF BRIGADE.

Major [George] Morgan,[47] W.	30	0	0	,,
Captain [Alexander] Irwin,[48] W.	,,	,,		
,, [Patrick] Gordon [49]	,,	,,		
,, [Hugh] Caldwell,[50] W.	,,	,,		
,, Henry Whitney [51]	,,	,,		
,, [Thomas] Whitney [52]	,,	,,		
Cornet [William] Ashby,[53] W.	,,	,,		

[1] Eldest son of Sir Winston Churchill. Born at Ashe in Devonshire, and baptized there June 28, 1650. The barest outline of the great Duke's military career is all that is possible here. He received an Ensigncy in the 1st Foot Guards 14 Sept. 1667. Capt. in the "Admiralty Regt." 10 June 1672. Is said to have served against the Moors as a volunteer at Tangier, but details are lacking. Appointed Capt. in the Duke of Monmouth's English Regt. in the service of France. Was distinguished for his gallantry at the sieges of Maestricht and Nimeguen in 1673, on which occasions he won the praise of Louis XIV. and the great Turenne. In 1674 commanded an English corps in the sanguinary engagement at Waldheim, near Strasburg, where 5 of his officers were killed. On his return to England was promoted Lt.-Col. of the Duke of York's Maritime Regt. 5 Jan. 1675. Colonel of a Regt. of Foot 17 Feb. 1678. Commanded a body of English troops in Flanders same year. Created Baron Churchill in 1682. Colonel of the Rl. Regt. of Dragoons 19 Nov. 1683. Second in command at the battle of Sedgemoor in July 1685. Colonel of the 3rd Tp. of Life Guards 1 Aug. 1685. Joined the Prince of Orange at the Revolution. Created Earl of Marlborough 9 April 1689, and sent over to Flanders same spring as Commander-in-Chief. Gained a victory over the French at the battle of Walcourt 15 Aug. 1689. Commanded a body of English, German, and Dutch troops at the reduction of Cork and Kinsale in Dec. 1690. Fell into disgrace with Wm. III. in 1691, and was not employed again in a military capacity until 1700, when he was appointed Commander-in-Chief of the British forces in Holland, and Ambassador to the States General.

Captain-General of all the British forces at home and abroad 10 March 1702. As Commander-in-Chief of the British, Dutch, and allied forces in Flanders, Marlborough began in 1702 that glorious career of uninterrupted success which justly earned for him the reputation of the greatest general of his time. An English dukedom and an Austrian princedom were bestowed on him, the former for the successes he gained in the campaign of 1702, and the latter for his victory at Blenheim. The pitched battles of Ramillies, Oudenarde, and Malplaquet added undying fame to Marlborough, and Queen Anne ordered a general thanksgiving after each of these three notable victories. One French stronghold after another was besieged and taken by the British and their allies. Among the captured fortresses of most importance were Lille, Tournay, Mons, Douay, and Bouchain. The last-named triumph closed Marlborough's military career (1711). He died 16 June 1722, and had a national funeral in Westminster Abbey. His remains were removed to Blenheim Palace in 1744. Colonel of the 3rd Troop of Life Guards and 1st Foot Guards; also Master-General of the Ordnance. He had been deprived of these posts and his captain-generalship in 1712, for political reasons, but was restored to his places on the accession of George I.

² 3rd son of Sir Winston Churchill. Born 2 Feb. 1756. Ensign in the Duke of York's Maritime Regt. in 1674. Lieut. 29 Oct. 1675. Capt. 8 Jan. 1678. Capt.-Lieut. of the Royal Dragoons 11 June 1679. Lieut.-Col. of the Tangier Regt. (now 4th Foot) 24 Apr. 1682. Went over to the Prince of Orange in Nov. 1688. Colonel of the 3rd Foot (Buffs) 31 Dec. 1688. Served at Tangier, Sedgemoor, Steinkirk, Landen (where he took his nephew, the Duke of Berwick, prisoner), Namur, Blenheim, and Ramillies. Major-General 2 March 1694. Lieut.-General 9 Mar. 1702. General of the Foot 15 Sept. 1703. Colonel of the Coldstream Guards 25 Feb. 1707. He held at different times the Governorship of Kinsale, Brussels, and Guernsey. Was Lieut.-Gov. of the Tower. Died 20 Sept. 1714, and was buried in Mintern church, Dorsetshire. M.I.

³ 2nd son of Richard Cutts of Childerley, Cambs. Served many years in Holland, and at the time of the Revolution was Colonel of an English Regt. in the service of the States-General (comn. dated 17 April 1688). Served through all William III.'s campaigns with distinction. Was created Baron Cutts of Gowran, co. Kilkenny, 12 Dec. 1690. He seemed to have a charmed life in battle, and led forlorn hopes on several occasions. He loved to fight in the deadly breach, and earned the *sobriquet* of "The Salamander." Brigadier-Gen. 22 March 1693. Col. of the Coldstream Guards 3 Oct. 1694. Maj.-Gen. 1 June 1696. Lt.-Gen. 11 Feb. 1703. Appointed Gen. of the forces in Ireland and a Lord Justice (1705) and d.s.p. 26 Jan. 1706. Buried in Christ Church Cathedral, Dublin. Cutts was a poet of no mean order. Steele, who served under Lord Cutts, dedicated his first and most deservedly-popular production, "The Christian Hero," to his lordship.

⁴ Only brother to Richard, Earl of Scarborough. Capt. in the Queen's Regt. of Horse (now King's Dragoon Guards) 13 June 1685. Lt.-Col. 31 Dec. 1688. Bt. Col. 1 Dec. 1689. Col. 10 Aug. 1692. Served with great distinction through all the wars of King William and Queen Anne. Brigdr.-Gen. 22 March 1693. Maj.-Gen. 27 Apr. 1697. Lt.-Gen. 11 Feb. 1703. Gen. of Horse 31 Jan. 1711. Resigned the command of his Regt. in 1717. Gov. of Jersey and an M.P. Died 18 Oct. 1722 aged 63, and was buried in a vault under Sawbridgeworth parish church. M.I.

⁵ Fifth son of Anne, Duchess of Hamilton, and Wm., Duke of Hamilton (so created in 1660) Born at Hamilton Palace, Lanark, and baptized there 9 Feb. 1666. Appointed Capt. in the Roya Scots Regt. of Foot 9 May 1684. Went over to William of Orange at the Revolution. Succeeded Col. Tho. Lloyd as Col. of an Enniskillen Regt. of Foot 1 Mar. 1690, and fought at the Boyne and at Aughrim. Was in every general action, and at most of the sieges, during the campaigns of William III. and Marlborough. Col. of the Rl. Fusiliers 23 Jan. 1692. Transferred to the Royal Scots 1 Aug. 1692. Created Earl of Orkney 3 Jan. 1696. His patent contains this clause:—"He has given many signal demonstrations of his fidelity and zeal, and of his courage and conduct both in the battles at the Boyne and Aughrim, Steinkirk and Landen, and at the sieges of Athlone and Limerick, and most eminently of late at the siege of Namur under his Majesty's own sight and observation." Brigdr.-Gen. 1 July 1695. Maj.-Gen. 9 March 1702. Lt.-Gen. 1 Jan. 1704. Knight of the Thistle. Gen. of the Foot 1711. Gov. of Virginia and of Edinburgh Castle. Representative Peer of Scotland. Premier Field Marshal 12 Jan. 1736. Died 29 Jan. 1737. Buried at Taplow.

⁶ Said to have been a son of Sir Geo. Ingoldsby, brother to Sir Hen. Ingoldsby. Major of the last-named officer's Regt. of Foot 8 March 1689. Served at the sanguinary action at Newry 24 Nov. 1689. Adjt.-Gen. to the Expedition sent to the French coast in 1692. Col. of the Regt. now known as the Rl. Welsh Fusiliers 28 Feb. 1693. Served at Namur. Brigdr.-Gen. 1 June 1696. Maj.-Gen. 9 March 1702. Lt. Gen. 1 Jan. 1704. Transferred to the Colonelcy of the Rl. Irish Regt. of Foot 1 Apr. 1705. A Lord Justice of Ireland and M.P. for Limerick. Married Frances Naper. Died in Dublin in Jan. 1712. Buried in Christ Church.

⁷ Brigdr. and eldt.-Lt. in 2nd Tp. of Life Guards 15 June 1685. Major of Col. Robt. Byerley's Regt. of Horse 12 Apr. 1690. Lt.-Col. of Col. Hugh Wyndham's Regt. of Carabiniers 31 Jan. 1692. Col. of a Regt. of Horse (now 3rd Dn. Gds.) 1 Dec. 1693. Brigdr.-Gen. 9 May 1702. Maj.-Gen. 1 Jan. 1704. Wounded at Schellenberg. Lt.-Gen. 1 Jan. 1707. Distinguished himself as a cavalry leader during the Irish campaign (1689-91), and in Flanders under Wm. III. and Marlborough. D. in May 1712. Said to have been the son of a Staffordshire clergyman, and having been unfortunate in commerce, enlisted as a private in Queen Catherine of Braganza's Tp. of Life Guards.

⁸ Lieut. in the Duke of Monmouth's Regt. of Foot 10 Feb. 1678. Sent to Tangier in 1679. Lieut in the Tangier Regt. of Foot 2 Oct. 1683. Capt.-Lieut. 1 Oct. 1688. Major of the Coldstream

Guards 10 Aug. 1692. Major of the 1st Ft. Gds. 25 Feb. 1695. Lt.-Col. of do. 7 Dec. 1696. Brigdr.-Gen. 9 Mar. 1702. Maj.-Gen. 1 Jan. 1704. Lt.-Gen. 1 Jan. 1707. Saw considerable service at Tangier and in Flanders. Distinguished himself at the taking of Tournay in 1709. D. 11 Nov. 1729. Bd. in Westmr. Abbey. M.I.

[9] Of Balnagowan. Son of the 11th Baron Ross. Cornet in the King's Own Royal Regt. of Scots Horse before 1688. Capt. in Col. Jas. Wynne's Regt. of Inniskilling Dragoons before July 1689. Lt.-Col. of last-named Regt. before 1694. Bt.-Col. 16 Feb. 1694. Regtal. Col. 16 July 1695. Brigdr.-Gen. 9 Mar. 1702. Maj.-Gen. 1 Jan. 1704. Lt.-Gen. 1 Jan. 1707. Col.-Gen. of all the Dragoon Forces 1 May 1711. Gen. 1 Jan. 1712. On 8 Oct. 1715 was removed from the command of his Regt. by George I., but was reappointed 1 Feb. 1729. D. at Bath 5 Aug. 1732. Bd. at Fearn in Ross-shire.

[10] Prior to the Revolution this officer served as Capt. in Lord Mountjoy's Regt. of Foot. Major of the Earl of Meath's Regt. of Foot 1 May 1689. Lt.-Col. of do. 1 Oct. 1690. Col. of do. 19 Dec. 1692. Served through the campaigns in Ireland and Flanders. Distinguished himself at the siege of Namur, where he was wounded, and where his Regt. had 1 Lt.-Col., 4 Capts., and 7 Subalterns killed and many officers wounded. Re-commissioned 1 Oct. 1695 as "Col. of the Royal Regt. of Foot of Ireland." Brigdr.-Gen. 9 Mar. 1702. Maj.-Gen. 1 Jan. 1704, but only recd. bounty as a Brigadier! Disposed of the Colonelcy of the Royal Irish in 1705, and d. a Lt.-Gen. His portrait is at Kilmainham Hospital, of which institution he was a Governor.

[11] Son of Col. Webb of Ribbesden Manor, Wilts. Appointed Cor. in the Queen's Regt. of Dragoons 2 Aug. 1685. Wounded in a skirmish at Wincanton between a party of King James's Cavalry and some troops of the Prince of Orange in Nov. 1688 (Boyer's *Life of Wm. III*.). Capt of Grendrs. in the first Ft. Gds. 1 Apr. 1689. Col. of the Regt. now known as the 8th (King's) Regt. of Foot 26 Dec. 1695. Brigdr.-Gen. 1 Jan. 1704. Maj.-Gen. 1 June 1706. Lt.-Gen. 1 Jan. 1709. Recd. the thanks of Queen Anne and Parliament for his victory over the French at Wynendael, near Lille, in 1708. Recd. a pension from Queen Anne, 27 March 1709, of "£1,000 per annum for 99 years if the Queen live so long." Wounded at Malplaquet. Governor of the Isle of Wight. Retained the Colonelcy of the 8th Foot until Aug. 1715. D. in 1724.

[12] Of Balmakellie. Third son of Wm. Ferguson of Badifurrow, Co. Aberdeen. Joined the Scots Brigade in Holland as Quarter-Master to Col. Macdonell's Regt. 12 June 1677. Capt. 1 Apr. (n. s.) 1688. Accompanied his Regt. (Lauder's) to England at the Revolution. Fought at Killiecrankie. Promoted Major after that battle. Comded. the troops sent against the Rebels in the Western Highlands in 1690. Lt.-Col. of Col. Andrew Monroe's Regt. of Foot (the Cameronians) 1 Aug. 1692. Served at Steinkirk and Landen. Col. of the Cameronians 25 Aug. 1693. Brigdr.-Genl. 9 Sept. 1703. Did good service both at Schellenberg and Blenheim. D. at Bois-le-Duc 22 Oct. 1705. Bd. in the choir of St. John's Church, Bois-le-Duc, M.I. Brigadier Ferguson was to have been promoted Maj.-Gen. on Marlborough's return to England in 1705.

[13] Joined the Royal Scots as Ens. 10 Nov. 1685. Capt. in Col. Robt. Hodges's Regt. of Foot 31 Dec. 1688. Major 1 Jan. 1692. Lt.-Col. 1 Oct. 1692. Col. of the Scots Fusiliers 1 Jan. 1697. Brigdr.-Gen. before Aug. 1704 (Comn. not forthcoming). Served at Steinkirk, Landen, and Namur. His Brigade led the attack on the village of Blenheim, and he headed his own Regt. with distinguished gallantry, advancing up to the enemy's palisades before giving the word "fire" (*Records*). He gloriously fell with the word of command on his lips. The Brigadier's wife (*née* Jean Johnson) d. at Edinburgh in child-birth, 19 June 1702, and was bd. in the Grey Friars cemetery, M.I. The Brigadier's children received £90 bounty money. One of them, Wm. Row, tho' still a child, was given a Comn. as 1st Lieut. in the Scots Fusiliers 25 Aug. 1704.

[14] Eldest son of Hen. Cadogan, Counsellor-at-Law, of Dublin, and grandson of Major Wm. Cadogan, Gov. of Trim, Co. Meath. Capt. in Brigdr.-Gen. Tho. Erle's Regt. of Foot 4 March 1694. Major of the Inniskilling Dragoons 1 Aug. 1698. Bt.-Col. of Foot 1 June 1701. Qr.-Mr.-Gen. 1 July 1701. Col. of the Regt. now known as the 5th Dragoon Guards 2 March 1703. Brigdr.-Gen. 25 Aug. 1704. Maj.-Gen. 1 Jan. 1707. Lt.-Gen. 1 Jan. 1709. Wounded at the siege of Mons same year. Col. of the Coldstream Guards 11 Oct. 1714. Transferred to the 1st Foot Guards 18 June 1722. Created Baron Cadogan 30 June 1716 and advanced to an earldom 8 May 1718. Was Marlborough's favourite general during his campaigns in Flanders and Germany. Cadogan was taken prisoner at the siege of Menin in 1706, but was soon after exchanged. Shared Marlborough's disgrace the last three years of Queen Anne's reign, but was restored to favour by Geo. I. Was second in command to the Duke of Argyll in Scotland at the close of the 1715 Rebellion. Master-Gen. of the Ordnance 18 June 1722. D. 17 July 1726. Failing issue, the earldom expired, but the barony of Cadogan passed according to limitation to the nephew of the deceased earl.

[15] Son of Arthur Meredyth of Dollardstown, Co. Meath. Appointed Capt. in the Duke of Leinster's Regt. of Horse 23 Apr. 1691. Bt.-Col. 1 June 1701. Adjt.-Gen. of the Forces same date. Col. of a Regt. of Foot in Ireland (37th Foot) 12 Feb. 1702. Brigdr.-Gen. 1 Jan. 1704. Wounded at Schellenberg. Maj.-Gen. 1 Jan. 1707. Gov. of Tynemouth Castle 20 Feb. 1707. Lt.-Gen. 1 Jan. 1709. Col. of the Scots Fusiliers 1 May 1710. Col. of the Regt. now known as the 20th Foot 4 Oct. 1714. He saw considerable service under Wm. III. and Marlborough. Gov. of Dendermond after its capitulation in 1706. Gentleman of the Horse to the Master of the Horse in 1708. Wounded at Oudenarde. M.P. for Midhurst in 1709. Died in 1719 and was bd. in St. Patrick's Cathedral, Dublin, on 19 June.

[16] A cadet of the old Yorkshire family of this name. Appointed Capt. in Lord Cavendish's Regt. of Horse (7th Dragoon Guards) 31 Dec. 1688. Lt.-Col. of Col. Hugh Wyndham's Regt. of Cara-

biniers 2 Jan. 1694. Col. of Horse 1 July 1702. Brigdr.-Gen. 1 Jan. 1704. Maj.-Gen. 1 Jan. 1707. Lt.-Gen. 1 Jan. 1709. Envoy to the Duke of Savoy in 1709. Held the Colonelcy of the Regt. now known as the 6th Dragoon Guards from 1 Oct. 1707—2 Apr. 1712. Transferred to a newly-raised Regt. of Dragoons 22 July 1715. D. at Dresden 4 Jan. 1719.

[17] Son of Lord John Hay, who succeeded in 1697 as 2nd Marquis of Tweeddale. Capt. in the Rl. Scots Dragoons 16 July 1689. Major 8 Sept. 1692. Lt.-Col., 28 Feb. 1694. Col. of Horse in 1702. In 1704 he purchased the Colonelcy of the Rl. Scots Dragoons from Visct. Teviot. Brigdr.-Gen. 1 Jan. 1704. Distinguished himself at Schellenberg, Blenheim, and Ramillies. Died of fever at Courtray 25 Aug. 1706.

[18] Only son of Dr. Robt. Spottiswood, Physician to the garrison at Tangier. Born at Tangier in 1676. Ens. in the Earl of Bath's Regt. of Foot 20 May 1693. Lieut. 1 Jan. 1696. Capt. 9 April 1703 (Comn. signed by Marlborough). Bt.-Lt.-Col. 1 Jan. 1707. Taken prisoner by the French in 1708. Served at Malplaquet. Appointed Dep. Gov. of Virginia in 1710. Held this post 12 years. Col. of a Regt. of Foot raised in America 26 Dec. 1739, and appointed Qr.-Mr.-Gen. of the British Forces sent to the West Indies with rank of Maj.-Gen., but died at Annapolis, Maryland, while attending to the embarkation, 17 June 1740. See Appleton's *Cyclopædia of American Biography*.

[19] Son of Adam de Cardonnel, a French Protestant. Was chief clerk at the War Office prior to his appointment as Secretary to the Captain-General. Countersigned all the commissions signed by Marlborough. Frequently mentioned in the *Marlborough Dispatches*. Amassed a considerable fortune, but not without strong suspicion of having taken bribes from army contractors. Died 22 Feb. 1719. Buried at Chiswick. His only daughter, Mary, married William, 1st Earl Talbot.

[20] Of King's College, Cambridge. Son of Ric. Hare, of Leigh, Essex. Tutor to the Marquis of Blandford, at whose death Marlborough appointed Hare one of the chaplains to Chelsea Hospital (9 Aug. 1703). Chaplain-General to the British Forces in Flanders in April 1704. Present at Schellenberg and Blenheim. Wrote a detailed account of the latter battle to Secretary Harley. D.D. in 1708. Was a spectator of the surrender of Bouchain, 13 Sept. 1711. When his patron's management of the war was called in question by his political opponents, Dr. Hare upheld Marlborough's conduct in *Letters to a Tory M.P. on the Management of the War*. Appointed Dean of Worcester in 1715. Dean of St. Paul's in 1726. Bishop of St. Asaph in 1727, and translated to the see of Chichester four years later. Died 26 April 1740.

[21] Name omitted in the MS. See p. 12, note 1.

[22] Name omitted in the MS. Mr. Tho. Gardiner was Surgeon of the Household, and was appointed Surgeon-General of the Army 1 Oct. 1701.

[23] Son of Rev. Ric. Watkins, of Whichford, co. Warwick. Of Christ Church, Oxford. In 1712 was appointed secretary to the British plenipotentiaries at Utrecht. Sometime secretary to the Duke of Ormonde. Died in March 1727, aged 61, and was buried in Westminster Abbey. The *Evening Post* of 30 March 1727 describes Watkins as "an upright, honest man." See Chester's *Westminster Abbey Registers*.

[24] Joined the Army as Ens. in the Duke of York's Maritime Regt., 16 Jan. 1678. Transferred to the 1st. Foot Guards, 17 April 1680. Lieut. 26 Jan. 1683. Capt.-Lieut. to Col. Jno. Berkeley's Regt. of Dragoons 17 July 1685. Capt. 31 Dec. 1688. Major 31 Mar. 1690. Lt.-Col. 1 Aug. 1692. Served at Steinkirk. Resigned his Comn. in the Cavalry 30 May 1696. Lt.-Gov. of Guernsey 10 April 1711.

[25] This officer's Christian name does not appear. A certain Capt. Jas. Fury accompanied the Earl of Peterborough to Spain in 1705, but in what capacity does not appear. See letter from Jas. Fury to the Lords of the Treasury, dated 11 Aug. 1715. *Treasury Papers*.

[26] Equerry to Prince George of Denmark, and A.D.C. to Marlborough at Ramillies, where his head was taken off by a cannon-ball as he was assisting the Duke on to his horse. Entered the Army as Cor. in Lord Shrewsbury's Regt. of Horse 27 Dec. 1685. Exempt and Capt. in the 1st Troop of Life Guards 1 Dec. 1693. Major of Horse in 1702. Comn. as Bt.-Lt.-Col. not forthcoming. Interred at Bavechem, Brabant. A monument was erected to his memory by his widow in Westminster Abbey. The Duchess of Marlborough was sent with a message of sympathy to Mrs. Bringfield by Queen Anne, and a promise of a pension for life. Luttrell's *Short Relation of State Affairs*, Vol. VI., p. 49.

[27] Appointed Capt. in the Queen's Regt. of Foot (4th Foot), 4 March 1693, Capt. in the 1st Foot Guards 6 Jan. 1703. Adjt.-Gen. of the Forces 25 Aug. 1704. Served at Ramillies and was sent in charge of four French generals and other prisoners to Nottingham. Brigdr.-Gen. 1 Jan. 1710. Col. of the Regt. now known as the 16th Foot 17 Feb. 1711. Died 1 Dec. 1712.

[28] Son of Col. Thomas Panton, of Charles II.'s Life Guards. Capt. in the Queen's Regt. of Horse, 20 Apr. 1695. Bt.-Lt.-Col. 25 Oct. 1703. Bt.-Col. 1 July 1706. Served at Malplaquet. Brigdr.-Gen. 12 Feb. 1711. Regtal.-Lt.-Col. in 1715. Attained the rank of Lt.-Gen. in 1735, and died 20 July 1753. It is related of this officer's father that he was a successful gamester, and "having in one night won a sum sufficient to ensure him an estate worth £1,500 a year, he never tempted fortune again, but acquired a positive aversion to both cards and dice." Chester's *Westminster Abbey Registers*, p. 214.

[29] Wm. Henry de Nassau, eldest son of the Earl of Rochford. This officer's name is omitted in the MS., but his bounty appears. The reason of the omission may be accounted for by the fact that Lord Tunbridge bore the second express from Marlborough to Queen Anne giving further particulars of

the victory of Blenheim, and the Queen presented Tunbridge with £1,000 (Luttrell's *Short Relation of State Affairs*, Vol. V., p. 457). Succeeded his father in 1708. Col. of a Regt. of Foot in 1706. Brigdr.-Gen. 1 Jan. 1710. Fell at the battle of Saragossa in Spain 27 July 1710.

[30] This officer's name is omitted in the MS., as he was the bearer of the first despatches from Marlborough to Queen Anne, announcing the victory of Blenheim, and received 1,000 guineas from her Majesty (Luttrell, Vol. V., p. 454). Son of a Virginian planter. Appointed Gov. and Capt.-Gen. of the Leeward Islands 25 Ap. 1706. On 7 Dec. 1710 a violent insurrection broke out in Antigua, the seat of government. Parke was murdered in his own house by the ringleaders, but he made a splendid defence, and killed Capt. Pigott, the chief leader of the insurrection, with his own hand.

[31] Natural son of General Chas. Churchill. Appointed Ens. in Prince Geo. of Denmark's Regt. of Foot 31 Dec. 1688. Capt. 1 Sept. 1697. Capt. in the Coldstream Guards 25 Oct. 1704. Major of the 3rd Foot 3 Apr. 1706. Bt-Col. 1 Jan. 1707. Col. of a Regt. of Foot, 25 March 1709. This corps was turned into Marines in Dec. 1709. Appointed Col. of a newly-raised Regt. of Dragoons in 1715. Gov. of Plymouth. Attained the rank of Lt.-Gen. 2 July 1739. Died in 1745. This officer obtained notoriety as the lover of the celebrated actress Anne Oldfield, by whom he had an illegitimate son, Charles Churchill.

[32] Appointed Capt.-Lieut. of Prince George of Denmark's Regt. of Foot 1 Jan. 1691. Capt. 14 Sept. 1693. Comn. renewed in 1702. Brevets of Major and Lt.-Col. not forthcoming. Bt.-Col. 1 Jan. 1707. Capt. and Lt. Col. in 1st Foot Guards before 1709. Served at Malplaquet. Regtal.-Major 11 Oct. 1722. Brigadier-General before 1722. Died in 1734.

[33] This officer's Christian name nowhere appears in the *Marlborough Dispatches* or other contemporary records. His identification with Lieut. Jno. Pitt of Major-Gen. Wood's Regt. of Horse is not established, as the said Lieut. was not promoted Capt. for some years after Blenheim. Capt. Pitt was A.D.C. to Marlborough at Ramillies, and was sent home with the despatches.

[34] This officer's real name was *Desaulnais*, but he Anglicised it to Disney, by which name he is better known. Appointed Ens. in the 1st Foot Guards 1 March 1694. Lieut. 15 Feb. 1703. Capt. in Prince Geo. of Denmark's Regt. of Foot before Aug. 1704. Capt. and Lieut.-Col. in 1st Foot Guards 11 March 1708. Appointed Col. of the Regt. now known as the 36th Foot 23 Oct. 1710. Served with the expedition to Canada in 1711. Transferred to the Colonelcy of the 29th Foot 25 Dec. 1725. D. 21 Nov. 1731. Buried in Westr. Abbey. M.I.

[35] Appointed 1st Lieut. of the Grendr. Cy. in Col. Jno. Gibson's Regt. of Foot 16 Feb. 1694. Served in Newfoundland in 1697. Capt. 20 Jan. 1698. Capt. in the Marquis de Puisar's Regt. of Foot 1 Aug. 1700. Capt. in Col. Wm. Watkins's Regt. of Foot 10 Aug. 1709. Placed on half-pay in 1713.

[36] This officer's name is spelt *Eaton* in some lists. Appointed Lieut. in Col. Cornelius Wood's Regt. of Horse 1 Apr. 1697. Capt 25 Aug. 1704. Served at Ramillies and Malplaquet. Bt.-Lt.-Col. 1 Jan. 1712. Served as Regtal. Major of aforesaid Regt. (now 3rd Dragoon Guards) in 1715. Promoted Lt.-Col. before 1 Jan. 1717. D. a few months afterwards.

[37] There is some doubt about this officer's identity. Fras. Scawen was a Lieut. and Capt. in the Coldstream Guards in 1704, and also held the rank of Quarter-Master. He was promoted Capt. and Lt.-Col. 3 Feb. 1705, and d. early in 1711.

[38] First Comn. as Ens. in the Royal Scots Regt. of Foot 29 May 1696. Placed on half-pay in 1697. Appointed Capt. of an additional Cy. in before-named Regt. 31 May 1701. Saw much service under Marlborough. A.D.C. to the Earl of Orkney at Blenheim. Particularly distinguished himself in this battle. Brevet-Major 1 July 1706. Bt.-Lt.-Col. 14 May 1709. Capt. and Lt.-Col in the Coldstream Guards in 1710. Sold his Comn. in last-named Regt., and bought the Lt.-Colonelcy of the Royal Scots Regt. of Foot 20 Mar. 1711. Bt.-Col. 1 Nov. 1711. Town Major of Dunkirk 24 Oct. 1712. Was created a Bart. in 1709 for his military services. D.s.p. in 1724.

[39] Second son of Mat. Pennefather, of the Tipperary family of this name. Appointed Ens. in Col. Ric. Ingoldsby's Regt. of Foot 1 June 1695. Lieut. 31 May 1701. Capt. before 25 Aug. 1704. Slightly wounded at Oudenarde. Bt.-Lt.-Col. 1 Jan. 1707. Appointed Commissary-Gen. of Ireland in May 1709. Auditor of the Irish Revenue in the reign of George I. M.P. for Cashel from 1716 until his decease in 1733.

[40] Entered the Army as Ens. in Brigdr.-Gen. Ric. Ingoldsby's Regt. of Foot 20 July 1696. Lieut. of the Grendr. Cy. 1 Feb. 1700. Wounded at Schellenberg. Capt. 24 Dec. 1704. Served at Ramillies and Malplaquet.

[41] Ens. in the Foot Guards 1 May 1693. 2nd Lieut. of Grenadiers, with rank of Captain 19 Apr. 1697. Capt. in the Rl. Irish Regt. of Foot 1 Nov. 1706. Major 8 June 1720. Lt.-Col. 4 Sept. 1734. D. 24 Apr. 1741.

[42] Cor. in the Queen's Regt. of Horse 1 June 1697. Lieut. and Bt.-Capt. 5 Aug. 1704. Served at Ramillies and Malplaquet. Serving in 1715.

[43] Cor. in the Queen's Regt. of Horse 1 June 1697. Lieut. before 13 Aug. 1704. Out of the Regt. in 1709.

[44] Cor. in Brigdr.-Gen. Cornelius Wood's Regt. of Horse 1 Oct. 1702. Lieut. 25 Aug. 1704. Served at Ramillies and Malplaquet. Comn. renewed in 1715. D. about 1716.

[45] Joined the Rl. Regt. of Dragoons of Ireland as a Qr.-Mr. in 1694. Cor. in the same Regt. 19 June 1702. Wounded at Schellenberg. Lieut. 23 Aug. 1707. Served at Malplaquet.

⁴⁶ Appointed A.D.C. to Marlborough in April 1704. Wounded by a shot in the leg at Schellenberg, and died shortly afterwards.

⁴⁷ Lieut. in Col. Toby Purcell's Regt. of Foot 17 Nov. 1692. Capt. 15 March 1695. Major in July 1704 (Comn. not forthcoming). Appointed Lt.-Col. of Col. Owen Wynne's newly-raised Regt. of Foot 25 March 1705. Out of last named Regt. before Apr. 1712.

⁴⁸ Joined the Royal Regt. of Foot 1 Oct. 1689. Adjt. to the 1st Batt. 22 May 1694. Capt. 2 Oct. 1695. Wounded at Schellenberg. Major 3 Aug. 1704. Served at Ramillies and Malplaquet. 1st Major of the Royal Scots Guards before 1715. Appointed Col. of the Regt. now known as the 5th Fusiliers 27 June 1737. Brigdr.-Gen. 1 Jan. 1743. D. a Lt.-Gen. in 1752.

⁴⁹ 2nd Lieut. of Grenadiers in the Royal Regt. of Foot 1 Oct. 1689. Capt. 3 Aug. 1694. Served under Wm. III. and Marlborough in Flanders. Out of the Regt. in 1709. On half-pay in 1714 as Major of Foot.

⁵⁰ Son of Sir Jas. Caldwell, Bt., of Castle Caldwell, Co. Fermanagh. Defended Donegal Castle against 2,000 dragoons under the Duke of Berwick in May 1689 (*Treasury Papers*, Vol. XXX. No. 25). Served in Flanders 1694–7. Major 1 Jan. 1703. Lt.-Col. of the Royal Regt. of Irish Dragoons 24 Apr. 1707. Bt.-Col. same year. Wounded at Schellenberg. Served at Ramillies and Malplaquet. Killed at the siege of Douay in 1710.

⁵¹ Ens. and Adjt. in the Princess Anne of Denmark's Regt. of Foot (8th Foot) 30 May 1696. Lieut. before 1702. Bt.-Capt. 25 Aug. 1703. Capt. in the Royal Regt. of Foot 3 Aug. 1704. Transferred to Col. Godfrey's Regt. of Foot 31 July 1708. Out of the Regt. in Jan. 1709.

⁵² Adjt. to Sir Jas. Lesley's Regt. of Foot 1 Aug 1690. Lieut. 12 Sept. same year. Capt. 10 Feb. 1695. Bt.-Major 1 July 1706. Served at Ramillies and Malplaquet. Bt.-Lt.-Col. 1 Jan. 1712. Appointed Lt.-Col. of Col. Tho. Chudleigh's Regt. of Foot (34th Foot) in 1715.

⁵³ Adjt. to Col. Cornelius Wood's Regt. of Horse 10 May 1694. Cor. 27 March 1699. Lieut. 25 Aug. 1704. Served at Ramillies and Malplaquet. Serving as Capt. in same Regt. in June 1727.

TRAIN OF ARTILLERY.*

COLONEL.

	£	s.	d.	
Holcroft Blood [1]	75	0	0	Bounty.

LIEUT.-COLONELS.

John [Henry] Hopeke [2]	60	0	0	,,
James Pendlebury [3]	60	0	0	,,

MAJOR.

Jonas Watson [4]	45	0	0	,,

CAPTAINS.

William Bousfield [5]	30	0	0	,,
Robert Guybons [6]	30	0	0	,,

LIEUTENANTS.

Peter Gelmuyden [7]	18	0	0	,,
Andrew Bonell [8]	18	0	0	,,

ADJUTANT.

Christopher Briscoe [9]	18	0	0	,,

QUARTER-MASTER.

Godfrey Franks [10]	18	0	0	,,

COMMISSARY OF DRAUGHT-HORSES.

Charles Ball [11]	18	0	0	,,

GENTLEMEN OF THE ORDNANCE.

Alexander [O']Hara [12]	12	0	0	,,
Edward French [13]	12	0	0	,,

ENGINEERS.

[Alex] Forbes [14]	16	10	0	,,
[Francis] Hawkins [15]	16	10	0	,,
[Hen.] Chaytor [16]	16	10	0	,,
[Chas.] Blount [17]	16	10	0	,,
[Richard] King [18]	16	10	0	,,
[Thos.] Lascelles,[19] W.	33	0	0	,,
[John] Armstrong [20]	16	10	0	,,

FIRE-WORKER.

Thomas Holman [21]	12	0	0	,,

COMMISSARY OF THE STORES.

John Fletcher [22]	18	0	0	,,

ASSISTANT COMMISSARIES.

John Carrey (sic) [23]	12	0	0	,,
John Bourden [24]	12	0	0	,,

BRIDGE-MASTER.

Thomas Marwood [25]	15	0	0	,,

MASTER-SURGEON.

	£	s.	d.	
John Girle [26]	20	0	0	Bounty.

ASSISTANT SURGEON.

John Pawlet [27]	9	0	0	,,
11 Conductors of Stores at	7	10	0	Each.
8 Sergeants at	7	10	0	,,
8 Corporals at	6	0	0	,,
8 Bombardiers at	6	0	0	,,
54 Gunners at	4	10	0	,,
6 more do., wounded, at	9	0	0	,,
53 Montrosses (sic) at	3	0	0	,,
3 more, wounded, at	6	0	0	,,
19 Pontoon men at	4	10	0	,,
1 do. man, wounded, at	9	0	0	,,
5 Master-Artificers at	12	0	0	,,
13 Artificers at	7	10	0	,,

* This Train was raised by Royal Warrant dated 14 March 1702. "The Confederates had 52 pieces of cannon in the field. Col. Blood distinguished himself by keeping the Enemy's foot in check with his nine field-pieces loaded with cartridge shot. Upwards of 100 cannon were taken from the enemy." *Cleaveland Notes,* p. 159.

¹ Son of Col. Thos. Blood, the would-be-thief of the Crown jewels in the reign of Chas. II. Served in his youth in the French Army, where he learnt the "engineering art." Returned to England in 1688, and was appointed Capt. of the Pioneers in Jas. II.'s Artillery Train. Served throughout the Irish campaign, and was wounded in action at Cavan in March 1690. Present at the taking of Cork and Kinsale. Appointed Capt. in Col. Jno. Foulkes's Regt. of Foot in 1692 and was ordered to the West Indies in Dec. 1692. It is a curious coincidence that a few days before Foulkes's Regt. was ordered to embark for the West Indies, Capt. Holcroft Blood was accused of being the person who had lately robbed the Portsmouth coach, and he was clapped into Winchester gaol and not allowed to sail with his regiment. The accused was set free in due course, having proved an *alibi,* and on 30 Oct. 1693 was promoted Major. Transferred as Major to Lord Cutts's Regt. of Foot 22 Mar. 1694. Served as Chief Engineer at Namur. This officer's plans for the defence of Bruges "against the insults of the French" in 1696 are still in existence (*King William's Sealed Bag,* 1696-7, No. 16, Public Record Office). Lt.-Col. of Sir Mat. Bridges's Regt. of Foot 7 July 1702. Brigdr.-Gen. 25 Aug. 1704. Col. of last-named Regt. 26 Aug. 1705. Commanded the Artillery at Ramillies and at the siege of Menin. D. at Brussels 30 Aug. 1707.

² Called "Hopkey" in most Lists. Served as Mate to the Fire-master in the 1689 Train. Appointed Fire-worker to Gen. de Ginkell's Train of Artillery in Ireland in 1691. Major of a Train of Ordnance to sail with the Fleet 1 May 1692. Received a similar appointment in 1694 and 1695. Major of the "Peace Train" 29 Nov. 1698. Lt.-Col. of the Artillery Train in Flanders 16 Feb. 1703 (Comn. signed by Marlborough). Lt.-Col. of the Artillery Train in Spain 1 Feb. 1707. First Col. of the Artillery in Holland 25 Mar. 1708. Received a similar appointment 10 Feb. 1711. Served at Malplaquet. Placed on half-pay in 1715. Brigdr.-Gen. 7 March 1727. D. in 1734, at which time he held the post of Comptroller of Fireworks.

³ Appointed Comptroller of the Peace Train 1 May 1698. Comptroller and Lt.-Col of the Artillery Train sent to Flanders in 1702. Chief Fire-master in 1706. 2nd Col. of the Artillery in Holland 25 Mar. 1708. Dep.-Gov. of the Tower of London 17 June 1709. Master-Gunner of England 20 Nov. 1710. 2nd Col. and Comptroller of the Artillery Train in Flanders 10 Feb. 1711. Half-pay as Colonel in 1715. Was Master-Gunner of England under three British sovereigns.

⁴ Appointed Capt. of an Artillery Company in the Flanders Train 1693. Senior Capt. of the Peace Train of 1698. Major of the Flanders Train — Feb. 1704. Major (with rank of Lt.-Col.) of the Artillery Train in Spain 18 Jan. 1707. First Lt.-Col. of Artillery in Holland 25 March 1708. Chief Bombardier 1 July 1710. First Lt.-Col. of Artillery in Holland 10 Feb. 1711. Lt.-Col. of the Royal Regt. of Artillery 17 March 1727. Comded. the Artillery at the defence of Gibraltar in 1727. Col. 10 July 1740. The following note on Col. Jonas Watson appeared in the *R. A. Proceedings,* July, 1898:—"There is a tradition that when the authorities called upon Colonel Watson to give the name of the best artillery officer he knew, for appointment to the command of the artillery of the expeditionary force sent to Carthagena (New Granada) at the end of 1740, he gave his own name. However this may be, he was appointed C.R.A., although he was 78 years of age. This fact was not overlooked by the writer of the scurrilous *Account of the Expedition to Carthagena, London,* 1743, who sneers at the uselessness of the 'poor gentleman' who was 'in his grand climaterick.' But the author of the sound and reliable *Journal of the Expedition to Carthagena, London,* 1744, shows that this imputation was as groundless as many other scandalous charges made by this anonymous libeller. ' Colonel Watson's merit and long service very justly entitled him to the command of the Train, . .

nor did his age ever prevent his attendance on duty, in the performance of which he lost his life by a shot which glanced from a tree at some distance from the Battery' (p. 56). The shot broke his thigh (*Gentleman's Magazine*, 1741, p. 268), and he died in April 1741."

[5] Raised himself by scientific ability and love of his profession from the humble rank of gunner to the proud position of Major of the Royal Regt. of Artillery, which post he held at the time of his death. In 1689 this officer was appointed a Gunner (Warrant Comn. dated 12 March 1689) to the Artillery detachment sent to the relief of Londonderry. In 1690-1 he served as a Bombardier in the Irish Train, receiving 2s. 6d. a day, and was at the Boyne, Aughrim, sieges of Galway and Limerick. Fought at Landen as a 2nd Lieut. in the Flanders Train, and was at the bombardment of Dieppe and Havre de Grace. Appointed Capt. in the Peace Train of 1698. Served at Ramillies and Oudenarde. Appointed Major in Holland in 1708. Served at the attack and capture of Vigo in 1719 as second in command of the Artillery. Major of the Royal Regt. of Artillery 8 Jan. 1730. D. at Greenwich 4 Dec. 1736.

[6] Appointed Lieut. of Pioneers in the Flanders Train of 1693. Served several campaigns in Flanders. Fire-master in the Peace Train of 1698. Capt. of a Cy. of Gunners in Flanders 1702-11. Out of the army in 1715.

[7] Appointed 2nd Lieut. in the Flanders Train of 1693. Served several campaigns under Wm. III. 1st Lieut. in the Peace Train of 1698. Served in Flanders 1702-12. Placed on half-pay as Captain in 1715.

[8] Appointed 2nd Lieut. in the Flanders Train of 1693. Served several campaigns under Wm. III. 2nd Lieut. in the Peace Train of 1698. Served in Flanders 1702-10. Capt. of a Cy. of Artillery in Flanders in 1710. Out of the Artillery in 1715.

[9] Appointed a Gentleman of the Ordnance in the Peace Train of 1698. Served in Flanders 1702-11. Was recommended by Brigdr.-Gen. Blood for the command of the Artillery Train in Portugal (*War Office M.S.*). Capt. of a Cy. of Artillery in Flanders in 1710. Capt. of a Cy. of Artillery at Gibraltar before 1717. Serving in last-named garrison in 1720.

[10] Served in Flanders 1702-10. 2nd Lieut. of the Artillery Train sent to Scotland in 1715. On half-pay as Lieut. in 1716.

[11] Served as Waggon-Master to the Flanders Train of Artillery in 1693, and greatly distinguished himself at the battle of Landen. Luttrell, under date of 15 Aug. 1693, says:—" Capt. Ball, an English officer who had the command of six pieces of cannon in the late fight, after most of the men had left the field, was attacked by the French, but he played the cannon so smartly on them that they retired, and he brought the six pieces of cannon to our camp; whereon he has kist the King's hand and is promised preferment" (Vol. III. p. 158). Appointed Waggon-Master-General by Comn. dated 1 Aug. 1693. This post was worth £100 per annum. Believed to have served at Ramillies and Malplaquet. Out of the Artillery 1 June 1711.

[12] Appointed a Gentleman of the Ordnance to the Flanders Train in 1702. Served throughout Marlborough's campaign. Appointed second Lt.-Col. of Artillery in Holland in 1708. Wounded at the siege of Mons in 1709. Chief Fire-worker in 1710. Out of the Army in 1715. This officer's real name appears to have been *O'Hara*. On 24 March 1705 he was appointed Capt. of a Cy. to be forthwith raised and added to the Rl. Regt. of Fusiliers, then commanded by Sr. Chas. O'Hara, who was created Baron Tyrawly in Jan. 1706. Out of the last-named Regt. in 1715.

[13] In 1688 this officer was serving as Master-Gunner at Tynemouth Castle. Appointed Lieut. of a Cy. of Artillery in Flanders before Dec. 1710. Out of the Artillery in 1715. Probably father to the Edwd. French appointed an Ens. in the Earl of Derby's Regt. of Foot 25 Aug. 1704.

[14] Served subsequently in the Barcelona Train. Appointed Engineer to the Expedition under Col. Fras. Nicholson sent to besiege Port Royal, Nova Scotia, in 1710. Present at the taking of Port Royal. Killed a few days later in action with a body of Indians. See Maj.-Gen. Porter's *Hist. of the Royal Engineers*, Vol. I. p. 137.

[15] Served subsequently in Spain, Newfoundland, and Jamaica. Placed on half-pay as Major in 1715.

[16] Eldest son of Sir Wm. Chaytor, Bt. (1st creation), of Croft, Co. Durham. Served four campaigns under Marlborough, and is said to have attained the rank of Major. Appointed Capt. *en second* in Col. Phineas Bowles's Regt. of Foot 5 March 1707. Predeceased his father, who d. in 1720.

[17] Son of Sir Thos. Blount, Bart. Served five years as an Engineer Officer in Flanders under Marlborough who procured him a Comn. as Capt. in Col. Heyman Rooke's Regt. of Foot in Sept. 1708 (*Dispatches*, Vol. IV. p. 235). Placed on half-pay in 1713. Killed in a tavern brawl in London in 1714.

[18] Served several campaigns under Marlborough and was appointed Colonel 12 Feb. 1710.. Col. of the Artillery Train sent to Canada with an Expedition commanded by Brigdr.-Gen. Jno. Hill in 1711. Qr.-Mr.-Gen. to the said Forces 1 March 1711. Serving as an Engineer on the old establt. in 1714, with pay at £100 per annum.

[19] Served several campaigns under Marlborough. Appointed Capt. in Major-Gen. Owen Wynne's Regt. of Foot. Placed on half-pay in 1713. D.-Qr.-Mr.-Gen. 22 Dec. 1712. Commissioner for demolishing the fortifications of Dunkirk in Sept. 1713, which fortress was surrendered to the British by the terms of the Treaty of Utrecht. Received £3 a day whilst employed at Dunkirk. Sent

to Scotland in 1715 on the outbreak of the Rebellion. On the death of Major-Gen. Jno. Armstrong 15 Apr. 1742, Col. Lascelles was appointed Surveyor-General and Chief-Engineer of Great Britain. Held these appointments until 1750, when he retired on account of his advanced age. D. in 1751, aged 80.

[20] Eldest son of Robert Armstrong of Ballyard, King's County. Bn. 31 March 1674. This distinguished Engineer served on Marlborough's Staff, and was A.D.C. to the Duke at Oudenarde. Also held for several years the post of Assistant-Qr.-Mr.-Gen. in Flanders. Greatly distinguished himself at the battle of Wynendale when conducting a convoy of 700 waggons from Ostend to Menin. A.D.C. to Marlborough at Malplaquet. Served at the sieges of Menin and Bouchain (mentioned and commended in Marlborough's despatches). Chief Commissioner for the demolition of the fortifications at Dunkirk. Received £3 a day whilst employed at Dunkirk. Qr.-Mr.-Gen. of the Forces *vice* Gen. Cadogan 22 Dec. 1712. Chief Engineer, with rank of Colonel in 1714. Held likewise the posts of Surveyor-Gen. of the Ordnance, Dep.-Lt.-Gen. of the Ordnance, Col. of the Royal Irish Regt. of Foot (13 May 1735—15 Apr. 1742) and was a Major-Gen. in the Army. D. at the Tower of London 15 Apr. 1742, and was bd. in the graveyard of the church within the Tower. M.I. See Burke's *Baronetage*, under "Armstrong of Gallen Priory, King's County."

[21] Appointed Gunner 30 Apr. 1680. Was sent with an Artillery detachment to the relief of Londonderry, with the rank of Master-Gunner in May 1689. Served several campaigns under Wm. III. and Marlborough in Flanders. Gentleman of the Ordnance in Flanders in 1710. Appointed a 1st Lieut. in the Royal Regt. of Artillery 26 May 1716. Capt.-Lieut. 1 Oct. 1721. Killed at the defence of Gibraltar 5 March 1727.

[22] Out of the Artillery before Dec. 1710.

[23] Called "Cazarice" in Kane's R.A. List (p. 104, edit. 1869). Serving in Flanders in 1710.

[24] Appointed a Gunner in the Artillery Peace Train of 1698. Out of the Artillery before Dec. 1710.

[25] Appointed a Gunner in the Artillery Peace Train of 1698. Served in Flanders from 1702–1712. Commissary of the Stores in 1710. Placed on half-pay as Capt. in 1715.

[26] Out of the Artillery before Dec. 1710.

[27] Serving in Flanders as Master-Surgeon to the Artillery in 1710. Accompanied the Artillery Train to Scotland in 1715. A certain Jno. Pawlet was appointed Surgeon to the 2nd Troop of Life Guards before 1717.

HOSPITAL.

PHYSICIAN-GENERAL.

	£	s.	d.	
Dr. [Thomas] Lawrence [1]	60	0	0	Bounty.

PHYSICIANS.

Dr. Oliphant [2]	45	0	0	,,
Dr. [Nathaniel] Ogle [3]	45	0	0	,,

DIRECTOR AND 2 CLERKS.

John Hudson [4]	75	0	0	,,

APOTHECARY-GENERAL.

Isaac Teale [5]	30	0	0	,,

APOTHECARIES.

William Orr [6]	15	0	0	,,
Theo. Deane [7]	15	0	0	,,

SURGEONS.

Thomas Wilson [8]	30	0	0	,,
Claudius Amyand [9]	30	0	0	,,
John Goldie [10]	15	0	0	,,
Robert Roddam [11]	15	0	0	,,
Andrew Grierson [12]	15	0	0	,,
Robert Lee [13]	15	0	0	,,
William Neilson [14]	15	0	0	,,
John Gibson [15]	15	0	0	,,
William Geneste [16]	15	0	0	,,

[1] Son of Jno. Lawrence of St. Ives, and grandson of Sir Jno. Lawrence, Knt., of same town. Appointed Physician-General to the army in Ireland 6 March 1689. First Physician to Queen Anne. Author of *Mercurius Centralis*. D. in 1714. From him descended the Lawrences of Studley and Hackfall, Yorkshire. *Gent.'s Mag.* for 1815, Pt. II., p. 17.

[2] Possibly Dr. Fras. Oliphant, who had been Surgeon to the Scots Foot Guards in the last reign.

[3] Of Kirkley Hall, Northumberland. Father of Sir Chaloner Ogle, Knt., Adml. of the Fleet, who was created a Bart. Dr. Ogle d. in 1736.

[4] Held this post throughout Marlborough's campaigns. There are several references to this officer in the *Marlborough Dispatches*.

[5] Appointed Apothecary-Gen. to the Army in Ireland 1 Nov. 1689. D. in March 1710. Luttrell, Vol. VI., p. 362.

[6,7] Untraced.

[8] "Died of the barbarous usage he received from the enemy in Flanders in 1711" (*Treasury Papers*, Vol. CXCIV. No. 65). His widow received a special pension of £30 per annum.

[9] Appointed Surgeon to the Queen's Regt. of Horse before 1 Jan. 1715. Recd. a pension of £200 a year in 1722. D. in 1740, at which time he held the appointment of Surgeon to George II.

[10] Appointed Surgeon to Col. Godfrey's Regt. of Foot 25 Aug. 1704. Out of said Regt. 3 Nov. 1708.

[11-13] Untraced.

[14] Appointed Director of Hospitals erected for the service of the British Forces in Portugal, 1 March 1709. On half-pay in 1714. D. in 1737.

[15] Appointed Surgeon to Sir Roger Bradshaigh's Regt. of Foot 12 Apr. 1706 by the Duke of Marlborough. *War Office M.S.*

[16] Served subsequently as a Surgeon in Spain, and was taken prisoner with Gen. Stanhope's troops at Brihuega in Dec. 1710. On 25 Aug. 1712 was still a prisoner in Spain. *S.P.D. Anne*, Bundle 23, fo. 83.

LIEUT.-GENERAL LUMLEY'S REGT. OF HORSE.*

Mem.— *The names of officers serving on the Staff are given in italics. For annotations see under Staff.*

COLONEL.

	£	s.	d.	
Henry Lumley	123	0	0	Bounty.

LIEUT.-COLONEL COMMANDING [AT SCHELLENBERG.]

| [Wm. Palmer, W.] | | | | |

LIEUT.-COLONEL COMMANDING [AT BLENHEIM.]

| Thos. Crowther [1] | 88 | 10 | 0 | ,, |

MAJOR.

| Jno. Deane [2] | 81 | 0 | 0 | ,, |

CAPTAINS.

Chris. Billingsley [3]	64	10	0	,,
Thos. Panton	64	10	0	,,
Jno. Morey [4]	64	10	0	,,
Pat. Lisle [5]	64	10	0	,,
Jas. Bringfield	64	10	0	,,
Wm. Goodwin [6]	64	10	0	,,

CAPT.-LIEUT.

LIEUTENANTS.

Chas. Wiseman [7]	45	0	0	,,
Peter Law	45	0	0	,,
Chas. Alexander [8]	45	0	0	,,
Ben. Bishop [9]	45	0	0	,,
Jas. Stalker [10]	45	0	0	,,
Robt. Wilson	45	0	0	,,
Thos. Stirrop [11]	45	0	0	,,
Roger Barton,[12] W.	90	0	0	,,

CORNETS.

Wm. Benbow [13]	42	0	0	,,
Jno. Usher [14]	42	0	0	,,
Thos. Jackson [15]	42	0	0	,,
Tristram Dillington [16]	42	0	0	,,
Nath. Law [17]	42	0	0	,,
Chas. Law,[18] W.	84	0	0	,,

QUARTER-MASTERS.

Wm. Shaw [19]	25	10	0	,,
Ant. Dodsworth [20]	25	10	0	,,
Nich. Hallman [21]	25	10	0	,,
Geo. Hartwell [22]	25	10	0	,,
Hen. Whitaker [23]	25	10	0	,,
Jno. Dodsworth [24]	25	10	0	,,
Jno. Scott [25]	25	10	0	,,
Fras. Kingston [26]	25	10	0	,,

CHAPLAIN.

| Jno. Gaile [27] | 20 | 0 | 0 | ,, |

THE BLENHEIM ROLL.

ADJT.

		£	s.	d.
Fras. Kingston [28]	- - - -	15	0	0 Bounty.

SURGEON.

| Alex. Inglis [29] | - - - - - | 18 | 0 | 0 | ,, |

[VOLUNTEER]

[Mat. Pitt [30]] - - - - -

* Now known as the King's Dragoon Guards. The non-commissioned officers and men who received bounty money were 27 corporals, each of whom received £2 10s., 17 trumpeters, 1 kettle-drummer, and 412 troopers, each of whom received £2.

[1] Entered the Army as Lieut. in the Duke of York's Maritime Regt. of Foot 30 March 1681. Cornet in the Queen's Regt. of Horse 28 July 1685. Capt. before 1689. Major 10 Aug. 1692. Bt.-Col. 1 Jan. 1704. Regtal.-Lt.-Col. 5 Aug. 1704. Commanded his Regt. at Schellenberg (after Bt.-Col. Wm. Palmer had been mortally wounded) and Blenheim. Brigdr.-Gen. 1 Jan. 1706. Served at Malplaquet. Major-Gen. 1 Jan. 1710. Left the Regt. on promotion to Maj.-Gen., but was reappointed Major to his former Regt. 27 July 1713, and was given a troop in the same corps 19 Apr. 1714, on resigning the Majority to Bt.-Major Jno. Morey. George I. renewed Maj.-Gen. Crowther's Comn. as Capt. in above Regt.

[2] Appointed Cornet in the Queen's Regt. of Horse 26 Sept. 1688. Capt. 17 June 1690. Bt.-Major 1 March 1703. Major 5 Aug. 1704. Bt.-Lt.-Col. 1 Jan. 1707. Served at Malplaquet. Out of the Regt. 27 July 1713.

[3] Appointed a Qr.-Mr. in the Queen's Regt. of Horse 10 June 1685. Lieut. in Lord Brandon's Regt. of Horse 1 Oct. 1688. Capt. in the Queen's Regt. of Horse 10 Aug. 1692. Served at the battle of Landen. Served throughout Marlborough's campaigns. Bt.-Major 1 Jan. 1706. Comn. renewed by George I.

[4] Appointed Capt.-Lieut. in the Queen's Regt. of Horse 14 Feb. 1694. Capt. 1 June 1697. Served throughout Marlborough's campaigns. Bt.-Major 1 Jan. 1707. Regtal.-Major 19 Apr. 1714. Comn. renewed by George 1.

[5] Appointed Lieut. in the Queen's Regt. of Horse 10 Aug. 1692. Capt.-Lieut. 9 Feb. 1699. Served at Landen and in several of Marlborough's campaigns. Capt. 25 Apr. 1703. Comn. renewed by George I.

[6] Appointed Lieut. in the Queen's Regt. of Horse 22 Aug. 1693. Comn. renewed in 1702. Capt.'s Comn. not forthcoming. Believed to have served at Ramillies. Out of the Regt. in 1709.

[7] Appointed Cornet in the Queen's Regt. of Horse 20 June 1696. Capt.-Lieut. in 1705 (Comn. not forthcoming). Capt. 24 June 1706. Served at Ramillies and Malplaquet. Out of the Regt. in 1714.

[8] Appointed Lieut. in the Queen's Regt. of Horse 9 Feb. 1695. Taken prisoner in a skirmish near Namur, 19 July 1695 (D'Auvergne's *Hist. of the Campaign of* 1695 *in Flanders*, p. 156). Capt.-Lieut. 24 June 1707. Served at Ramillies and Malplaquet. Out of the Regt. in 1714.

[9] Appointed Cornet in the Queen's Regt. of Horse 9 Feb. 1695. Lieut. 24 May 1702. Served at Ramillies and Malplaquet. Comn. renewed by George I.

[10] Appointed Lieut. in the Queen's Regt. of Horse 25 Apr. 1703. Served at Ramillies and Malplaquet. Transferred to Lt.-Col. Deane's Tp. in same Regt., with the rank of Capt. 14 March 1712. Resigned his Comn. about 1716.

[11] Appointed Cornet in the Queen's Regt. of Horse 12 June 1694. Lieut. 9 Feb. 1699. Served at Ramillies. Killed at Malplaquet.

[12] Appointed Lieutenant in the Queen's Regt. of Horse 20 Sept. 1695. Left the Regt. 24 May 1708.

[13] Appointed Cornet in the Queen's Regt. of Horse 25 March 1704. Lieut. 24 May 1708. Served at Ramillies and Malplaquet. Capt. before Jan. 1715.

[14] Appointed Cornet in the Queen's Regt. of Horse 24 June 1700. Out of the Regt. in 1708.

[15] Appointed Cornet in the Queen's Regt. of Horse 22 Aug. 1693. Lieut. 24 June 1707. Served at Ramillies and Malplaquet. Out of the Regt. before 1 Jan. 1715.

[16] Appointed Ens. in the 1st Foot Guards 12 June 1701. Succeeded his half-bro. John as Bart. of Knighton. Cornet in the Queen's Regt. of Horse 24 Apr. 1703. Bt.-Capt. 24 June 1707. M.P. for Newport, Isle of Wight, in 1707. Appointed Lt.-Col. *en second* of Col. Jos. Wightman's Regt. of Foot 5 March 1708. Transferred to the Coldstream Guards as Capt. and Lt.-Col. before 1710. 2nd Major to last-named Regt. 12 Aug. 1717. D. 4 July 1721.

[17] Appointed Adjt. to the Queen's Regt. of Horse 22 Aug. 1694. Cornet 20 Sept. 1695. Left the Regt. about 1705.

[18] Appointed Adjt. to the Queen's Regt. of Horse 26 March 1699. Cornet's Comn. not forthcoming. Lieut. 24 Sept. 1677. Served at Ramillies and Malplaquet. Comn. renewed by George I. Called " Laws " in some Lists.

[19] Serving as Qr.-Mr. in same Regt. in 1709. Further services untraced. A certain Wm. Schaw was appointed Adjt. to Sir Chas. Hotham's Regt. of Foot 12 Apr. 1710.

[20] Cornet in same Regt. 24 May 1708. Served several campaigns under Marlborough. Out of the Regt. in 1715.

[21] Serving as Qr.-Mr. in same Regt. in 1709. Further services untraced.

[22] Out of the Regt. in 1708.

[23] Serving as Qr.-Mr. in same Regt. in 1709. Further services untraced.

[24] Appointed Adjt. to the Queen's Regt. of Horse 24 Sept. 1705. Cornet 24 June 1707. Comns. renewed by George I.

[25] Out of the Regt. in 1708.

[26] Cornet in same Regt. 24 Sept. 1705. Serving as Lieut. in 1715.

[27] Appointed Chaplain 10 March 1702. Serving as Chaplain in the same Regt. in 1709. Left the Regt. 27 July 1714.

[28] Resigned the Adjutancy 24 Sept. 1705. See note 26.

[29] Appointed Surgeon to Chelsea Hospital 16 March 1707.

[30] "A gentleman of a good family in Somersetshire, well affected, and hath good interest to raise men; hath served a campaign in Germany in Lt.-Gen. Lumley's Regt. of Horse, prays to be an ensign" (Recommendation for a Comn. by Lt.-Gen. Lumley in 1706. *War Office MS.*). Further services untraced.

MAJOR-GENERAL WOOD'S REGT. OF HORSE.*

COLONEL.

	£	s.	d.	
Cornelius Wood, W.	246	0	0	Bounty.

LIEUT.-COL. COMMANDING.

[Jno. Featherstonhalgh,[1] K.]

MAJOR.

[Somerford] Oldfield [2]	81	0	0	,,

CAPTAINS.

[Phil.] Armstrong,[3] W.	129	0	0	,,
Saml. Shute,[4] W.	129	0	0	,,
[Chas. Carrington,[5] K.]				

CAPT.-LIEUT.

Edwd. Whaley [6]	45	0	0	,,

LIEUTENANTS.

Thos. Hull [7]	45	0	0	,,
Jno. Pitt [8]	45	0	0	,,
Thos. Armstrong [9]	45	0	0	,,
Jas. Eyton	45	0	0	,,
Thos. Dove [10] W.	90	0	0	,,

CORNETS.

[Thos.] Hicks [11]	42	0	0	,,
[*Geo.*] *Stephenson*, W.	84	0	0	,,
[Fras.] Forrester,[12] W.	84	0	0	,,
[Chas. Odiarne,[13] K.]				
Wm. Ashby, W.	84	0	0	,,

QUARTER-MASTERS.

Jno. Munt [14] (*sic*)	25	10	0	,,
[Hugh] Magennis [15]	25	10	0	,,
— Ricketts [16]	25	10	0	,,
— Chapman [17]	25	10	0	,,
— La Chapelle [18]	25	10	0	,, .
[David] Lawrence, [19] W.	51	0	0	,,

CHAPLAIN.

[Geo.] Child [20]	20	0	0	,,

ADJT.

Geo. Stephenson, W.	15	0	0	,,

SURGEON.

Jas. Goodwin [21]	18	0	0	,,

* Now known as the 3rd Dragoon Guards. The non-commissioned officers and men who received bounty money were 16 corporals, each of whom received £2 10s.; 12 trumpeters, 1 kettle-drummer, and 259 troopers, each of whom received £2.

[1] Of Stanhope Hall, Durham. Appointed Capt. of an Indep. Tp. of Horse 20 June 1685. After Sedgemoor this Tp. was incorporated into the Earl of Arran's Regt. of Cuirassiers. Major of Col. Cornelius Wood's Regt. of Horse 10 Feb. 1694. Lt.-Gov. of Carlisle 17 Dec. 1697. Lt.-Col. of Wood's Horse 1 July 1702. Col. of Horse 1 Jan. 1704. His widow received £177 Bounty money.

² Appointed Capt. in Visct. Colchester's Regt. of Horse 14 June 1691. Major 1 July 1702. Left the Regt. as Lt.-Col. in 1707.

³ Eldest son of Edmund Armstrong (See Burke's *Baronetage* under "Armstrong of Gallen"). Appointed Lieut. in the Marquis de Miremont's Regt. of Horse 22 Sept. 1688. Capt.-Lieut. in Visct. Colchester's Regt. of Horse 14 June 1690. Capt. 1 Sept. 1691. Received £250 by Rl. Warrant, dated 3 Apr. 1695, "in consideration of wounds received by him at the battle of Landen, and losses." Major's Commission not forthcoming. Bt.-Lt.-Col. 1 Jan. 1707. Lt.-Col. 8 Aug. 1707. Served several campaigns under Marlborough. D. at Ghent unmarried in Nov. 1711, aged 70.

⁴ Appointed Capt. in Col. Thos. Windsor's Regt. of Horse 16 Feb. 1694. Bt.-Major in Wood's Regt. 1 Jan. 1707. Major 24 Aug. 1707. Regtal.-Lt.-Col. before 1715. Bt.-Col. 16 Oct. 1712. Governor of Massachusetts 1716-1723. D. 15 Apr. 1742, aged 80.

⁵ Appointed Capt.-Lieut. in Visct. Colchester's Regt. of Horse 10 Aug. 1692. Capt. 31 March 1697. Killed at the battle of Schellenberg. Bounty of £120 to his widow and children.

⁶ Appointed Lieut. in Visct. Colchester's Regt. of Horse 1 Aug. 1692. Capt.-Lieut. 1 April 1697 Capt. 1 Aug. 1704. Served several campaigns under Marlborough, and left the Regt. 23 Apr. 1709.

⁷ Appointed Lieut. in Col. Cornelius Wood's Regt. of Horse 1 Apr. 1697. Capt. 24 Aug. 1707. Bt.-Major 1 Jan. 1712. Served several campaigns under Marlborough. Comn. renewed by George I. Regtal.-Major about 1716. Regtal.-Lt.-Col. 2 Sept. 1720. Serving in 1730. Out of the Regt. in 1736.

⁸ Appointed Cornet in Lord Berkeley's Regt. of Horse 25 Feb. 1693. Lieut. 27 March 1699. Capt.-Lieut. 24 Aug. 1707. Capt. before 1715. Served several campaigns under Marlborough. Appointed Capt. in Col. Thos. Pitt's Regt. of Horse in 1715. Transferred to the 1st Foot Guards as Capt. and Lt.-Col. 5 June 1717. Governor of Bermuda 1727-1737. M.P. for Hindon, Camelford, and Old Sarum. Youngest son of Thos. Pitt, Gov. of Fort St. George, and bro. to Col. Thos. Pitt, Gov. of Jamaica, who was created Earl of Londonderry in 1726. Lt.-Col. Jno. Pitt d. in 1744.

⁹ Younger bro. to Capt. Philip Armstrong of above Regt. Appointed Cornet in Col. Cornelius Wood's Regt. of Horse 16 Feb. 1694. Lieut. 1 July 1702. Capt. about 1716. Resigned his Comn. in 1717. D. 7 Jan. 1748 aged 86. See Burke's *Baronetage* under "Armstrong of Gallen Priory, King's County."

¹⁰ Appointed Cornet in Princess Anne of Denmark's Regt. of Horse prior to 1693. Cornet in Col.-Thos. Windsor's Regt. of Horse in 1694. Lieut. in Brigdr.-Gen. Cornelius Wood's Regt. of Horse 10 July 1702. Left the Regt. 24 Dec. 1708.

¹¹ Erroneously called "William" Hicks in the MS. Appointed Cornet in the above Regt. 1 June 1704. Lieut. 24 Dec. 1708. Served several campaigns under Marlborough. Comn. renewed by George I.

¹² Appointed Cornet in the Earl of Arran's Regt. of Horse 16 Feb. 1694. Cornet in Brigdr.-Gen. Wood's Regt. of Horse 10 July 1702. Lieut. 24 Aug. 1707. Serving in Flanders in 1709. Out of the Regt. in 1715.

¹³ Appointed Cornet in Col. Cornelius Wood's Regt. of Horse 16 Feb. 1694. Bounty of £84 for his widow and children.

¹⁴ Out of the Regt. in 1708.

¹⁵ Serving in Flanders in 1694 as a Qr.-Mr. in Col. Cornelius Wood's Regt. of Horse. Cornet 16 July 1705. Served at Malplaquet. Out of the Regt. in 1715.

¹⁶ Serving in Flanders in 1694 as a Qr.-Mr. in Col. Wood's Regt. of Horse. Out of the Regt. in 1708.

¹⁷ Do.

¹⁸ Not in any subsequent List.

¹⁹ Served previously as Qr.-Mr. in Col. Thos. Windsor's Regt. of Horse. Promoted Cornet 24 Aug. 1706. Out of the Regt. 24 Feb. 1708.

²⁰ Appointed Chaplain to Visct. Colchester's Regt. of Horse 29 Aug. 1691. Out of the Regt. in 1708.

²¹ Appointed Surgeon 1 June 1703. Out of the Regt. 24 Dec. 1708.

BRIGADIER-GENERAL CADOGAN'S REGT. OF HORSE.*

COLONEL.

	£	s.	d.	
Wm. Cadogan	123	0	0	Bounty.

MAJOR COMMANDING.

| [Robt.] Napier [1] | 88 | 10 | 0 | ,, |

CAPTAIN.

| [Geo.] Fletcher [2] | 64 | 10 | 0 | ,, |

CAPT.-LIEUT.

| [Jas.] Fleming [3] | 45 | 0 | 0 | ,, |

LIEUTENANTS.

| [Jas.] Farrer [4] | 45 | 0 | 0 | ,, |
| [Jno. Henry Grueber,[5] K.] | | | | |

CORNETS.

[Metcalf] Graham [6]	42	0	0	,,
[Daniel] Crispin [7]	42	0	0	,,
[Jno.] Macmahon [8]	42	0	0	,,

QUARTER-MASTERS.

[Jno.] Crosby [9]	25	10	0	,,
—— Spence [10]	25	10	0	,,
[Jno.] Garston [11]	25	10	0	,,

ADJT.

| [Jno.] Macmahon [12] | 15 | 0 | 0 | ,, |

SURGEON.

| [Daniel] Cabrole [13] | 18 | 0 | 0 | ,, |

* Only three Troops of this Regt. (now known as the 5th Dragoon Guards) were present at Blenheim. The non-commissioned officers and men who received bounty money were 6 corporals, each of whom received £2 10s.; 6 trumpeters and 123 troopers, each of whom received £2.

[1] Called "Napper" in most Lists. Appointed Capt. in Col. Jno. Coy's Regt. of Horse 20 Jan. 1692. Major 14 Apr. 1702. Bt.-Lt.-Col. 25 Aug. 1704. Bt.-Col. 1 June 1706. Was at the forcing of the French lines in 1705, and at the battles of Ramillies and Malplaquet. Brigdr.-Gen. 12 Feb. 1711. Col. of above Regt. 27 May 1717. Maj.-Gen. in 1727. Lt.-Gen. in 1735. D. 10 Nov. 1739.

[2] Appointed Capt. in Col. Jno. Coy's Regt. of Horse 21 Jan. 1692. Bt.-Lt.-Col. 25 Aug. 1704. Served throughout Marlborough's campaigns.

[3] Appointed Lieut. in above Regt. before 1702. Capt.-Lieut. 14 Apr. 1702. Bt.-Capt. 25 Aug. 1704. Capt. 2 Apr. 1708. Served throughout Marlborough's campaigns. Bt.-Lt.-Col. of Horse 1 Jan. 1712.

⁴ Appointed Lieut. in Col. Jno. Coy's Regt. of Horse 1 March 1692. Bt.-Capt. 1 Sept. 1704. Serving in Flanders in 1709.

⁵ Appointed Cornet in Col. Jno. Coy's Regt. of Horse 1 March 1692. Lieut. 14 Apr. 1702. Killed at Blenheim. Bounty of £90 to his widow.

⁶ Son of Reginald Graham, who was 4th son of Sir Geo. Graham, Bt., of Esk, Cumberland. Appointed Cornet in above Regt. 14 Apr. 1702. Bt.-Capt. 1 Sept. 1704. Capt.-Lieut. 2 Apr. 1708. Served as A.D.C. to Marlborough at Ramillies, Malplaquet, &c. Several of his letters from the seat of war are preserved at Levens Hall, Westmoreland. Bt.-Lt.-Col. 14 May 1709. Was sent home with despatches after the battle of Malplaquet. Appointed Adjt.-Gen. to the British Forces in Flanders, 19 Feb. 1711, with rank of Colonel of Horse.

⁷ Appointed Cornet in the Earl of Arran's Regt of Horse 25 March 1700. Lieut. 25 Aug. 1704. Called "Crespiner" in the *Flanders Army List* for 1709.

⁸ Appointed a Qr.-Master in Col. Jno. Coy's Regt. of Horse 1 Apr. 1689. Cornet 15 Apr. 1702. Resigned the Adjutancy 24 Aug. 1705. Serving as Cornet in 1709.

⁹ Called "Crossly" in his Comn. as Qr.-Mr. in above Regt., dated 1 June 1690. Appointed Adjt. 24 Aug. 1705. Serving in Flanders in 1709.

¹⁰ Out of the Regt. in 1708.

¹¹ Appointed a Qr.-Mr. in Col. Jno. Coy's Regt. of Horse 1 March 1689. Cornet 25 Aug. 1704. Latter Comn., which was signed by Marlborough, is in the Editor's possession. Left the Regt. 24 Feb. 1709.

¹² See note 8.

¹³ Appointed Surgeon to Brigdr.-Gen. Ingoldsby's Regt. of Foot 2 July 1696. Surgeon to the Earl of Arran's Regt. of Horse 19 May 1700. Serving in Flanders in 1709.

LIEUT.-GENERAL WYNDHAM'S REGT. OF HORSE.*

LIEUT.-COLONEL COMMANDING.

	£	s.	d.	
Fras. Palmes	123	0	0	Bounty.

MAJOR.

[Phil. Chenevix,[1] K.]

CAPTS.

| [Jno.] Petry [2] | 64 | 10 | 0 | ,, |
| Wm. Windham,[3] W. | 129 | 0 | 0 | ,, |

CAPT.-LIEUT.

| [Geo.] Robinson [4] | 45 | 0 | 0 | ,, |

LIEUTENANTS.

[Wm.] Guyon [5]	45	0	0	,,
[Wm.] Payne,[6] K.]				
[Wm.] Kyrle,[7] W.	90	0	0	,,
Chas. Hall,[8] W.	90	0	0	,,
[Ric.] Edmonds,[9] W.	90	0	0	,,

CORNETS.

[Ric. Saunders,[10] K.]				
[Jas.] Harrison [11]	42	0	0	,,
[Thos.] Scaife,[12] W.	84	0	0	,,
[Thos.] Newell,[13] W.	84	0	0	,,
[Clifton Thomson,[14] K.]				
[Ric.] Ward, [15]	84	0	0	,,

QUARTER-MASTERS.

[—— Crocker,[16] K.]				
[Ric.] Beswick [17]	25	10	0	,,
[Wm.] Finley [18]	25	10	0	,,
[Jno.] Lowick [19]	25	10	0	,,
[Jno.] Gatford [20]	25	10	0	,,
[Geo.] Baker [21]	25	10	0	,,

CHAPLAIN.

| [Walter] Wells [22] | 20 | 0 | 0 | ,, |

ADJT.

[Clifton Thomson,[23] K.]

SURGEON.

| [Wm.] Stone [24] | 18 | 0 | 0 | ,, |

---

* Now known as the 6th Dragoon Guards (the Carabiniers). The non-commissioned officers and men who received bounty money were 17 corporals, each of whom received £2 10s.; 12 trumpeters, 1 kettle-drummer, and 256 troopers, each of whom received £2. Lieut.-Gen. Wyndham was serving in Portugal, hence his absence from his Regt.

[1] Son of the Rev. Philip Chenevix, Protestant pastor of Limay, near Nantes. Appointed Brigadier and Eldest Lieut. in the 1st Tp. of Life Guards 20 Apr. 1689. Served at the Boyne and in Flanders. Appointed Major of Col. Hugh Wyndham's Regt. of Carabiniers, 3 Dec. 1700. Bounty of £162 to his widow and 3 children in 1705.

[2] Appointed Adjt. and Youngest Lieut. of the 2nd Tp. of Life Guards, 1 June 1689. Brigadier and Eldest Lieut. 1 Nov. 1690. Major of the Earl of Arran's Regt. of Horse 16 Feb. 1694. Placed on

half-pay in 1697. Capt. in Brigdr-Gen. Hugh Wyndham's Regt. of Carabiniers in 1702. Major 1 Oct. 1706. Bt.-Lt.-Col. 1 Jan. 1707. Bt.-Col. 15 Nov. 1711. Served several campaigns under Marlborough.

[3] One of the younger sons of Wm. *Windham*, of Felbrigge, Norfolk, by Katherine, dau. of Sir Jos. Ashe, Bart. Appointed Cornet in his kinsman Hugh Wyndham's Regt. of Carabiniers, 12 March 1698. Capt. 22 Sept. 1702. Regtal.-Lt.-Col. 10 Oct. 1706. On half-pay in 1714. Had his leg amputated after Blenheim. The following letter from Capt. Windham to his mother is in the possession of R. W. Ketton, Esq., of Felbrigge Hall :—" Nordlingen, Aug. 23, o.s. 1704. I was loth to write very soon after my first account I gave you of my being shot in the leg in the late engagement, because truly my surgeons could not tell well what to think of the matter; but upon my arrival at this place—which is the hospital for all our wounded—I have got all the help I can desire, and on Tuesday last was a fortnight my leg was doomed to be cut off, and accordingly was that day, since which time I thank God there has not happened the least ill accident that could be . . . . Surely a greater victory [Blenheim] was never gained. They were 11,000 foot stronger and we were 5,000 stronger in horse. They were so strongly encamped that they laughed to see us coming." Served at Ramillies and Malplaquet. D. about 1740.

[4] Appointed Lieut. in Col. Hugh Wyndham's Regt. of Carabiniers, 26 Feb. 1694. Capt.-Lieut. 20 Feb. 1698. Bt.-Capt. 1 Oct. 1702. Capt. 25 Aug. 1704. Bt.-Major 1 Jan. 1707. Served throughout Marlborough's campaigns.

[5] Appointed Cornet in Col. Robert Byerley's Regt. of Horse 25 Jan. 1692. Lieut. 20 May 1695. Capt. 1 Oct. 1708. Served throughout Marlborough's campaigns.

[6] Appointed Lieut. in Col. Hugh Wyndham's Regt. of Carabiniers 26 Feb. 1694. His widow received £90 bounty money in 1705.

[7] Appointed Lieut. in Col. Robt. Byerley's Regt. of Horse 2 July 1691. Capt. 25 Aug. 1704. Served throughout Marlborough's campaigns. Out of the Regt. 23 Jan. 1712.

[8] Appointed Cornet in Col. Hugh Wyndham's Regt. of Carabiniers 14 Sept. 1693. Lieut. 20 Feb. 1698. Out of the Regt. in 1709.

[9] Appointed Cornet in Col. Hugh Wyndham's Regt. of Carabiniers 26 Feb. 1694. Lieut. 1 Apr. 1704. Served throughout Marlborough's campaigns.

[10] Appointed Cornet to the Colonel's Tp. in Col. Hugh Wyndham's Regt. of Carabiniers 22 March 1695.

[11] Appointed Cornet in above Regt. in 1702 (Comn. not forthcoming). Lieut. 24 Feb. 1706. Served throughout Marlborough's campaigns.

[12] Appointed Adjt. to the Queen's Regt. of Dragoons 15 May 1702. Cornet in Lt.-Gen. Wyndham's Regt. of Carabiniers before August 1704. Lieut. 25 Aug. 1704. Served throughout Marlborough's campaigns.

[13] Appointed Cornet in Col. Thos. Windsor's Regt. of Horse 16 Feb. 1694. Placed on half-pay in 1697. His Comn. as Cornet in the Carabiniers is not forthcoming. Out of last-named Regt. in 1708.

[14] Appointed Cornet in Col. Hugh Wyndham's Regt. of Carabiniers 20 May 1695. Adjt. 10 March 1702. Bounty of £114 to his widow and 2 children in 1705.

[15] Appointed Cornet in Col. Hugh Wyndham's Regt. of Carabiniers 5 July 1696. Capt.-Lieut. of Lt.-Gen. Farrington's Regt. of Foot 23 Nov. 1710. On the half-pay list as Capt. in 1714.

[16] Untraced.

[17] Date of Comn. not forthcoming. Serving in 1709 as a Qr.-Mr. in above Regt.

[18] Date of Comn. not forthcoming. Promoted Cornet 24 Feb. 1706. Serving in Flanders in 1709.

[19] Date of Comn. not forthcoming. Promoted Cornet 24 Feb. 1708. Serving in Flanders in 1709.

[20] Date of Comn. not forthcoming. Promoted Lieut. 24 Aug. 1704. Serving in Flanders in 1709.

[21] Date of Comn. not forthcoming. Promoted Lieut. 1 Oct. 1706. Serving in Flanders in 1709.

[22] Appointed Chaplain to Col. Hugh Wyndham's Regt. of Carabiniers 15 Aug. 1698. Serving in Flanders in 1709.

[23] See note 14.

[24] Appointed Surgeon to above Regt. 10 March 1702. Serving in Flanders in 1709.

THE DUKE OF SCHOMBERG'S REGT. OF HORSE.*

LIEUT.-COLONEL COMMANDING.

	£	s.	d.	
Chas. De Sybourg [1]	123	0	0	Bounty.

MAJOR.

[Ric. Creed,[2] K.]

CAPTAINS.

Phil. Prime,[3] W.	129	0	0	,,
Ric. Coote [4]	64	10	0	,,
Robt. Norton [5]	64	10	0	,,

CAPT.-LIEUT.

| Ric. Pope [6] | 45 | 0 | 0 | ,, |

LIEUTENANTS.

Jno. Looker [7]	45	0	0	,,
Molineux Robinson [8]	45	0	0	,,
Stephen Palmes,[9] W.	90	0	0	,,
Claude Têtefolle,[10] W.	90	0	0	,,
[Saml. Hawkes,[11] K.]				

CORNETS.

Jno. Reeves [12]	42	0	0	,,
Jno. Clarke,[13] W.	84	0	0	,,
Jno. Cruseau,[14] W.	84	0	0	,,
Archd. Little,[15] W.	84	0	0	,,

QUARTER-MASTERS.

[——— Charlton,[16] K.]				
Ben. Colson [17]	25	10	0	,,
Ric. Deane [18]	25	10	0	,,
Robt. Lyth [19]	25	10	0	,,
Peter Boyer [20]	25	10	0	,,
[——— Kelsall,[21] K.]				

CHAPLAIN.

| Dr. Wells [22] | 20 | 0 | 0 | ,, |

ADJT.

| Ben. Colson [23] | 15 | 0 | 0 | ,, |

SURGEON.

| Chas. Le Roy [24] | 18 | 0 | 0 | ,, |

---

* Now known as the 7th Dragoon Guards. The non-commissioned officers and troopers who received bounty money were 11 corporals, each of whom received £2 10s., and 235 troopers (including trumpeters), each of whom received £2. The Duke of Schomberg was commanding the British forces in Portugal in the summer of 1704, hence his absence from his Regt.

[1] Is said to have been an illegitimate son of Meinhardt, Duke of Schomberg. Appointed Major of above Regt. 1 May 1694. Lt.-Col. 1 March 1703. Bt.-Col. 1 Jan. 1704. Commanded above Regt. at Schellenberg, Blenheim, and Ramillies. Brigdr.-Gen. 1 Jan. 1707. Commanded a Brigade at Oudenarde. Maj.-Gen. 1 Jan. 1710. Col. of a Regt. of Foot (late Orrevy's) 8 Dec. 1710. Col. of his former Regt. (now 7th D. G.) 12 Oct. 1713. Gov. of Fort William in Scotland in Apr. 1725. D. a Lt.-Gen. 25 Jan. 1733, and was bd. in Westminster Abbey.

[2] Appointed Capt. in the Earl of Denbigh's Regt. of Dragoons 16 Feb. 1694. Capt. in the Duke of Schomberg's Regt. of Horse 1 March 1702. Major's Comn. not forthcoming. Killed in his third

charge at Blenheim. A monument was erected to his memory in Westminster Abbey. "It was erected by his mother, near another which her son, while living, used to look up to with pleasure, for the worthy mention it makes of that great man, the Earl of Sandwich, to whom he had the honour to be related, and whose heroic virtues he was anxious to emulate." Dean Stanley's *Memorials of Westminster Abbey*, p. 254.

[3] Erroneously called "Prince" in some of the MS. Lists. Appointed Lieut. in Lord Cavendish's Regt. of Horse 31 Dec. 1688. Capt.-Lieut. 1 Jan. 1694. Capt. 2 Apr. 1697. This officer is mentioned in a letter from Capt. Ric. Pope to Thos. Coke, dated 16 Aug. 1704, giving an account of the battle of Blenheim (Earl Cowper's MSS. printed by the *Hist. MSS. Comn.*, Vol. III., p. 40). Out of the Regt. in 1705.

[4] Appointed Capt. in above Regt. 1 March 1703. Served at Ramillies and Malplaquet.

[5] Appointed Adjt. in Lord Cavendish's Regt. of Horse 31 Dec. 1688. Capt.-Lieut. 2 Apr. 1697. Capt. in 1702. Major 25 Aug. 1704. Bt.-Lt.-Col. 1 Jan. 1707. Col. of Horse 15 Nov. 1711. Served throughout Marlborough's campaigns.

[6] Appointed Cornet in Lord Cavendish's Regt. of Horse before 10 Apr. 1689. Lieut. 23 Apr. 1691. Capt.-Lieut. in 1702. Capt. 25 Aug. 1704. Bt.-Major 1 Jan. 1707. Left the Regt. 2 Apr. 1711. Served throughout Marlborough's campaigns. Had his horse shot under him at Schellenberg and Blenheim. There are some interesting letters from this officer to his cousin Thos. Coke, Esq., M.P., in the possession of Earl Cowper, at Melbourne Hall, Derbyshire, which letters have been printed by the *Hist. MSS. Comn.* (12th Report, Appx. Part III.). The following extract from Pope's letter to T. Coke, dated "Dillingen, 16 Aug. 1704," refers to the campaign of 1704:—"I did not give you an account of the affair of Schellenberg, because it appeared to me with a different face to what it did over all Europe, it being in my opinion a considerable advantage, purchased at a dear rate, rather than a victory. But this last [battle], that my Lord Tunbridge brings you an account of, is the greatest and most glorious action that has happened in several ages, to the immortal glory of the Queen's arms, to the perpetual fame of my Lord Duke, who exposed himself as much as any officer or soldier in the army, and much more than most of the generals. As to the number the enemy has lost 'tis probable they will never be so ingenuous to publish—'tis so great, they lie so dispersed that we cannot compute it." *Earl Cowper's MSS.*, Vol. III., p. 40.

[7] Appointed Cornet in above Regt. 22 Nov. 1696. Lieut. 25 March 1703. Bt.-Capt. 6 Apr. 1708. Capt.-Lieut. 2 Apr. 1711. Served throughout Marlborough's campaigns.

[8] Appointed Cornet in above Regt. 1 Apr. 1694. Lieut. 2 Apr. 1697. Capt.-Lieut. 25 March 1705. Capt. 24 Feb. 1708. Served throughout Marlborough's campaigns. Comn. renewed by George I. and George II.

[9] Appointed Cornet in above Regt. 23 Apr. 1691. Lieut. in 1702. Capt. 25 March 1705. Bt.-Major 1 Jan. 1712. Served throughout Marlborough's campaigns.

[10] Appointed Cornet to the Duke of Schomberg's own Tp. in above Regt. 9 May. 1694. Lieut. 15 Feb. 1699. Capt.-Lieut. 24 Feb. 1708. Capt. 2 Apr. 1711. Served throughout Marlborough's campaigns. Attained the rank of Major. Living in 1727. See *Treasury Papers*, Vol. CCLXII., No. 2.

[11] Appointed Cornet in above Regt. 25 May 1691. Lieut. 1 Apr. 1694. £90 Bounty money to his widow and 3 children.

[12] This officer's Comn. as Cornet is not forthcoming. Out of the Regt. in 1708. Probably son of Jno. Reeves of same Regt., whose Comn. as Capt. was dated 2 Apr. 1697.

[13] Appointed Cornet to the Duke of Schomberg's own Tp. in above Regt. 15 Feb. 1699. Lieut. 25 March 1705. Out of the Regt. 11 May 1708.

[14] A Huguenot. Appointed Cornet in above Regt. 28 Jan. 1696. Out of the Regt. in 1708.

[15] Called "Arthur Little" in the MS. Appointed Cornet in above Regt. 2 Apr. 1697. Out of the Regt. in 1708.

[16] This officer's Comn. as Qr.-Mr. is not forthcoming, nor does his Christian name appear in any List. He was probably son of Capt. John Charlton, late of the same Regt., who belonged to an old Derbyshire family of this name. £51 Bounty money to his widow.

[17] Promoted Cornet in above Regt. 24 Aug. 1707. Resigned the Adjutancy same date. Served throughout Marlborough's campaigns.

[18] Serving as Qr.-Mr. in above Regt. in 1709.

[19]   Do.

[20]   Do.

[21] This officer's Comn. of Qr.-Mr. is not forthcoming. £51 Bounty money to his widow and 2 children.

[22] Out of the Regt. before 25 June 1705. Probably Theodore Wells appointed Chaplain to Col Owen Wynne's newly-raised Regt. of Foot 25 March 1705.

[23] See note 17.

[24] Appointed Surgeon to above Regt. 1 Jan. 1703. Serving in Flanders in 1709.

LORD JOHN HAY'S REGT. OF DRAGOONS.*

COLONEL.

	£	s.	d.	
Lord John Hay - - - -	105	0	0	Bounty.

LIEUT.-COL. COMMANDING.

| [Geo.] Preston [1] - - - - | 78 | 10 | 0 | ,, |

MAJOR.

| And. Agnew [2] - - - - - | 61 | 10 | 0 | ,, |

CAPTAINS.

Ninian Boyd [3] - - - -	46	10	0	,,
[Tho. Young,[4] K.] - - - -				
[Jno.] Stewart [5] - - - -	46	10	0	,,

CAPT.-LIEUT.

| [Pat.] Robertson [6] - - - - | 27 | 0 | 0 | ,, |

LIEUTENANTS.

[Gideon] Keith [7] - - - -	27	0	0	,,
[Chas.] Preston [8] - - - -	27	0	0	,,
[Geo.] Skene [9] - - - -	27	0	0	,,
[Wm. Douglas,[10] K.] - - - -				
[Tho.] Mallard,[11] W. - - - -	54	0	0	,,

CORNETS.

[Wm.] Crauford [12] - - - -	24	0	0	,,
[Jas.] Livingston [13] - - - -	24	0	0	,,
[Maurice] Hill [14] - - - -	24	0	0	,,
[Alex.] Grant [15] - - - -	24	0	0	,,
[Archd.] Wilson [16] - - - -	24	0	0	,,

QUARTER-MASTERS.

[Jas.] Dudgeon [17] - - - -	16	10	0	,,
[Jas.] Douglas [18] - - - -	16	10	0	,,
[Geo.] Lauder [19] - - - -	16	10	0	,,
[And.] Fraine [20] - - - -	16	10	0	,,
[Jas.] Stewart [21] - - - -	16	10	0	,,
[Geo.] Armstrong [22] - - - -	16	10	0	,,

ADJT.

| [Jas.] Scott [23] - - - - | 15 | 0 | 0 | ,, |

SURGEON.

| [Jas.] Nisbet [24] - - - - | 18 | 0 | 0 | ,, |

GUNSMITH AND MATE.

| ——— - - - - | 15 | 0 | 0 | ,, |
| ——— - - - - | 15 | 0 | 0 | ,, |

* The Royal Scots Greys. The non-commissioned officers and troopers who received bounty money were 10 sergeants, each of whom received £2 10s.; 17 corporals, each of whom received £2; 288 troopers (including drummers and hautboys), each of whom received £1 10s. At Schellenberg 7 troopers were killed and 17 wounded.

[1] Appointed Capt. in the Rl. Scots Dragoons 8 Sept. 1692. Bt.-Lt.-Col. 1 Aug. 1702. Regtal.-Major 1 Apr. 1704. Regtal.-Lt.-Col. same year (Comn. not forthcoming). Col. 1 Jan. 1706. Sold

his Lt.-Colonel's place 24 Aug. 1706. Appointed Col. of the Cameronians 24 Aug. 1706. Wounded at the battle of Ramillies. Commanded his Regt. at Malplaquet. Brigdr.-Gen. 12 Feb. 1711. Gov. of Nieuport 19 May 1713. Lt.-Gen. 2 July 1739. This distinguished soldier was younger son of Sir Geo. Preston, Bt., of Valleyfield, Co. Perth. Was Deputy-Governor of Edinburgh Castle in the reigns of George I. and II. On the outbreak of the '45 Rebellion, Lt.-Gen. Preston, then in his 86th year, proceeded at once to Edinburgh Castle, which he held for the King until the insurrection was over. The Government thought it necessary to despatch Lt.-Gen. Guest to Edinburgh to take over the supreme command, but it is generally believed that had it not been for Preston's strength of character, and his unceasing vigilance, General Guest would have surrendered the Castle to the Stuart forces after the battle of Preston Pans. It is recorded of Preston that "every two hours a party of soldiers wheeled him in an arm-chair round the guards that he might personally see if all were on the alert" (Grant's *Memoirs of the Castle of Edinburgh*, p. 171). This splendid old veteran died on 7 July 1748 aged 88.

² Eldest son of Alex. Agnew of Lochryan, Wigtownshire. Appointed Lieut. in the Royal Regt. of Scots Dragoons 17 Sept. 1689. Capt.-Lieut. 8 Sept. 1692. Capt. 22 March 1693. Bt.-Major 25 Apr. 1704. Regtal.-Major same year. Served at Ramillies. Bt.-Lt.-Col. Sold his Comn. 24 Aug. 1706. There is a letter extant from this officer to his cousin Sir Andrew Agnew, Bt., of Lochnaw, dated 28 Aug. 1693, *re* the purchase of a grey horse, which helps to establish the fact that the Scots Greys were mounted on grey horses at the date quoted (See *The Agnews of Lochnaw*, by Sir A. Agnew, Bt., p. 453). Lt.-Col. A. Agnew md. in 1700 his cousin Margaret Agnew, of Lochnaw; and secondly, Agnes, dau. of Sir T. Kennedy, Knt., of Kirkhill.

³ Appointed Lieut. in above Regt. 1 Oct. 1694. Capt.-Lieut. 28 Apr. 1697. Capt. before Aug. 1704. Major 24 Aug. 1706. Served at Ramillies and Oudenarde. Left the Regt. 24 March 1709.

⁴ Appointed Capt. in above Regt. 28 Apr. 1697. D. of wounds received at the battle of Schellenberg. Bounty of £93 to his widow and children.

⁵ This officer's Comn. as Capt. is not forthcoming. Out of the Regt. in 1706.

⁶ Erroneously called "Robinson" in the MS. and *Records*. Appointed Cornet in the Rl. Scots Dragoons 31 Dec. 1692. Lieut. in 1702. Capt. 10 Jan. 1707. Served throughout Marlborough's campaigns. Commanded a Troop of the Greys at Sheriffmuir and was wounded in that battle. It is related in the *Records of the Scots Greys* that prior to the battle of Sheriffmuir the Earl of Mar attempted to seduce some of the officers and men of the Greys from their allegiance, employing a lady to carry a letter to Captain Robertson. This underhand scheme proved fruitless. Promoted Major 27 May 1717. Major Robertson commanded three Troops of the Greys in an action at Strachell, Ross-shire, on 10 June 1719, when General Wightman defeated a body of Spaniards and Highlanders who had raised the Jacobite flag.

⁷ Appointed Cornet in the Rl. Scots Dragoons 8 Feb. 1694. Lieut. 4 May 1702. Bt.-Capt. 1 Jan. 1707. Served at Ramillies. Out of the Regt. 24 Feb. 1708.

⁸ Appointed Cornet to Major Preston's Tp. in the Rl. Scots Dragoons 4 May 1702. Lieut's. Comn. not forthcoming. Capt. 24 Aug. 1706. Served throughout Marlborough's campaigns. Out of the Regt. in 1715.

⁹ Appointed Cornet in the Rl. Scots Dragoons 28 Feb. 1694. Lieut. 4 May 1702. Capt. 16 Jan. 1707. Left the Regt. as Capt. and Bt.-Major 31 May 1715. Acted as Agent for the Earl of Stair (Col. of the Scots Greys 1706–1714) in London for some years. See letter from Major Skene to Lord Stair, dated "London, Apr. 18, 1718," in Graham's *Annals of the Viscount and 1st and 2nd Earls of Stair*, Vol. II. Appx. p. 381.

¹⁰ Appointed Lieut. in the Rl. Scots Dragoons 28 Apr. 1697. Killed at Schellenberg. Called Capt. in the Records of the Scots Greys.

¹¹ Appointed Lieut. in the Rl. Scots Dragoons in 1702. Wounded at Schellenberg. Brevet to act as Capt. in the Army 25 Aug. 1704. Brevet to take rank as Capt. in the Regt. 10 Jan. 1707. Served at Ramillies and Malplaquet. Out of the Regt. in 1715.

¹² Appointed Cornet in the Rl. Scots Dragoons 1 Oct. 1694. Capt.-Lieut. 16 Jan. 1707. Capt. of an additional Tp. in same Regt. 24 Feb. 1708. Served throughout Marlborough's campaigns. Transferred with his Tp. to Col. Wm. Kerr's newly-embodied Regt. of Dragoons (7th Hussars) in 1715.

¹³ Kinsman to Viscount Teviot, who was many years Colonel of above Regt. Appointed Cornet to the Colonel's Tp. in the Rl. Scots Dragoons 3 May 1702. Lieut. 11 May 1705. Served throughout Marlborough's campaigns. Capt. before 1713. Appointed Capt. in Col. Kerr's newly embodied Regt. of Dragoons (7th Hussars) 31 Jan. 1715.

¹⁴ Appointed Cornet in the Rl. Scots Dragoons 4 May 1702. Out of the Regt. before 1708.

¹⁵ From this officer's petition to Marlborough, in 1706, for a Cy. in the New Levies, it appears that he served as a Capt. of Foot in the last reign, and was reduced in 1697. Was given a Cornetcy in the Rl. Scots Dragoons by Lord Teviot, and served at Schellenberg and Blenheim (*War Office MS.*). Left above Regt. in 1706.

¹⁶ Appointed Adjt. to the Rl. Scots Dragoons 6 July 1697. Cornet's Comn. not forthcoming. Out of the Regt. in 1708.

[17] Serving as Qr.-Mr. in above Regt. in 1709. Out of the Regt. in 1713.
[18] Serving as Qr.-Mr. in above Regt. in 1713.
[19] Serving as Cornet in above Regt. in 1713. Comn. renewed by George I. Transferred as Cornet to Col. Kerr's Regt. of Dragoons in 1715.
[20] Serving as Qr.-Mr. in above Regt. in 1709. Out of the Regt. in 1713.
[21] Appointed Cornet in above Regt. 10 July 1706. Serving in 1709. Out of the Regt. in 1713. A certain Jas. Stewart was appointed Cornet in the Inniskilling Dragoons 19 Aug. 1715, and resigned his Comn. in 1716.
[22] Appointed Lieut. in above Regt. 16 Jan. 1707. Comn. renewed by George I.
[23] Promoted Lieut. 24 Feb. 1708. Wounded at Malplaquet. Out of the Regt. in 1713.
[24] Served throughout Marlborough's campaigns. Comn. renewed by George I.

MAJOR-GENERAL ROSS'S REGT. OF DRAGOONS.*

COLONEL.

	£	s.	d.	
Chas. Ross	105	0	0	Bounty.

LIEUT.-COLONEL COMMANDING.

| Owen Wynne [1] | 78 | 10 | 0 | ,, |

MAJOR.

| Robt. Hunter [2] | 61 | 10 | 0 | ,, |

CAPTAINS.

Jno. Hill [3]	46	10	0	,,
Ric. Gore [4]	46	10	0	,,
Hugh Caldwell, W.	93	0	0	,,

CAPT.-LIEUT.

| Robt. Drury [5] | 27 | 0 | 0 | ,, |

LIEUTENANTS.

Chas. Beatty [6]	27	0	0	,,
Jno. Johnston [7]	27	0	0	,,
Mat. Watts [8]	27	0	0	,,
Danl. Boisragon [9]	27	0	0	,,

CORNETS.

Jno. Dunbar [10]	24	0	0	,,
[Alex.] Abercromby [11]	24	0	0	,,
Jas. Hamilton [12]	24	0	0	,,
Jas. Poé [13]	24	0	0	,,
Jno. Hunter, [14] W.	48	0	0	,,
Edwd. Hamilton, W.	48	0	0	,,

QUARTER-MASTERS.

—— Brown [15]	16	10	0	,,
[Geo.] Mackean [16]	16	10	0	,,
[Ric.] Johnston [17]	16	10	0	,,
Ric. Dunbar [18]	16	10	0	,,
Jno. Skelston, [19] W.	33	0	0	,,
David Ross, [20] W.	33	0	0	,,

CHAPLAIN.

| Simon Babe [21] | 20 | 0 | 0 | ,, |

ADJT.

| David Ross, [22] W. | 30 | 0 | 0 | ,, |

SURGEON.

| Wm. Cocksedge [23] | 18 | 0 | 0 | ,, |

---

* The Royal Irish Dragoons, which were disbanded in 1798, but resuscitated in 1858 as the 5th Royal Irish Lancers. The non-commissioned officers and troopers who received bounty money were 12 sergeants, each of whom received £2 10s.; 18 corporals, each of whom received £2; and 268 dragoons (including drummers and hautboys), each of whom received £1 10s. At Schellenberg 4 troopers were killed and 19 wounded.

[1] Son of Owen Wynne and younger bro. to Brigdr.-Gen. Jas. Wynne, the former Colonel of above Regt. Appointed Major of the Rl. Irish Dragoons 1 Nov. 1694. Lt.-Col. 20 July 1695. Colonel of

a newly-raised Regt. of Foot 25 March 1705. Brigdr.-Gen. 1 June 1706. First Colonel of the Regt. now known as the 9th Lancers 22 July 1715. Transferred to the Colonelcy of the 4th Dragoon Guards 6 July 1719. Col. of the Rl. Irish Dragoons 6 Aug. 1732. D. a Lieut.-Gen. in 1737, at which time he was in command of the Forces in Ireland.

[2] Son of Jas. Hunter of the Hunterston family (Paterson *Hist. of Ayr and Wigtown*, Vol. III., p. 354). Appointed Aide-Major to Lord Cardross's Dragoons 19 Apr. 1689. Capt. in the Rl. Scots Dragoons 28 Feb. 1694. Brigade-Major to the Dragoons in Flanders 28 May 1695. Major of the Rl. Irish Dragoons 23 Apr. 1698. Bt.-Lt.-Col. 1 Jan. 1703. Served at Ramillies. Appointed Gov. of Virginia in 1708. Taken prisoner by the French on his way to America, but was soon afterwards exchanged for the Bishop of Quebec, then a prisoner in the hands of the English (Luttrell's *Diary*, Vol. VI., p. 336). Gov. of New York in 1709. Brigdr.-Gen. 12 Feb. 1711. Gov. of Jamaica 20 June 1729, and appointed Major-General. D. in Jamaica 31 March 1734. There is a memoir of Gen. Hunter in the *Dict. of Nat. Biog.*, but his early services and Comns., as given above, are omitted from said memoir. Is said to have had a command at the siege of Derry in 1689.

[3] Appointed Capt. in above Regt. 6 Nov. 1694. Regtal.-Major 24 April 1707. Bt. Lt.-Col. 1 Jan. 1707. Served throughout Marlborough's campaigns. Bt.-Col. 1 Nov. 1711.

[4] Ninth son of Sir Fras. Gore, Knt., of Artaman, co. Sligo. Appointed Capt. in above Regt. 1 Apr. 1695. Bt.-Major 1 Jan. 1707. Bt. Lt.-Col. 1 Nov. 1711. Served throughout Marlborough's campaigns.

[5] Appointed Lieut. in above Regt. before 1694. Capt. 25 March 1705. Bt.-Major 1 Nov. 1711. Served throughout Marlborough's campaigns.

[6] Appointed Lieut. in above Regt. 20 July 1695. Capt.-Lieut. 24 Feb. 1708. Served at Ramillies and Malplaquet.

[7] Appointed Lieut. in above Regt. 8 Dec. 1692. Capt.-Lieut. 25 March 1705. Capt. of an additional Tp. in same Regt. 24 Feb. 1708. Served at Ramillies and Malplaquet.

[8] Joined above Regt. as Cornet 20 July 1689, and served in the Irish campaign. Adjt. 20 June 1696. Lieut. 1 Nov. 1702. Served at Ramillies. Left the Regt. in 1708.

[9] Appointed Lieut. in above Regt. 8 May 1695. Out of the Regt. before 1709. One of this family was appointed Major to the Earl of Galway's Regt. of Dragoons in Ireland 24 Feb. 1709.

[10] Appointed Capt.-Lieut. in Col. Owen Wynne's newly-raised Regt. of Foot 25 March 1706. Capt. same date. Major 15 Oct. 1711. Appointed Major of Maj.-Gen. Owen Wynne's newly-raised Regt. of Dragoons (9th Lancers) in 1715.

[11] Joined above Regt. as a Qr.-Mr. before 1694. Promoted Cornet 20 July 1696. Lieut. 25 March 1705. Served at Ramillies and Malplaquet.

[12] Appointed Cornet in above Regt. 25 Apr. 1704. Lieut. 24 Feb. 1708. Served at Ramillies and Malplaquet.

[13] Called "Powe" in some Lists. 3rd son of Emanuel Poé, of co. Tipperary. Joined above Regt. as Qr.-Mr. before 1694. Promoted Cornet 19 June 1702. Lieut. to an additional Tp. in above Regt. 24 Feb. 1708. Served at Ramillies and Malplaquet. D. 1728.

[14] Joined above Regt. as Qr.-Mr. before 1694. Promoted Cornet 1 Nov. 1702. Lieut. to an additional Tp. in above Regt. 24 Feb. 1708. Served at Ramillies and Malplaquet.

[15] Not in any previous or subsequent List.

[16] Appointed Qr.-Mr. before 1703. Promoted Cornet 25 March 1705. Served at Ramillies and Malplaquet.

[17] Appointed Qr.-Mr. to above Regt. before 1704. Serving in Flanders in 1709.

[18] Do.

[19] Called "Skelton" in one List. Appointed Qr.-Mr. to above Regt. before 1704. Acted as Adjt. when Adjt. Ross was wounded until he also received a severe wound. Is put among the officers who were killed at Blenheim in Cannon's *Records of the 1st Dragoon Guards* (p. 32). Promoted Cornet 23 Aug. 1707. Serving in Flanders in 1709.

[20] Appointed Qr.-Mr. to above Regt. before 1703. Served as Adjt. at Blenheim until he was severely wounded. Out of the Regt. before 23 Aug. 1707.

[21] Called "Samuel Babbe" in the MS. Serving with the Regt. in Flanders in 1709.

[22] See note 20.

[23] Appointed Surgeon to above Regt. before 1694. Resigned his post of Surgeon 25 March 1705 and was appointed Cornet in same Regt. 25 March 1705. Served at Ramillies and Malplaquet.

THE FIRST REGT. OF FOOT GUARDS.*
1st BATT.

COLONEL.

	£	s.	d.	
John, Duke of Marlborough	117	0	0	Bounty.

LIEUT.-COL.

| Henry Withers | 85 | 10 | 0 | ,, |

MAJOR.

CAPTAINS.

[Gilbert] Primrose,[1] W.	99	0	0	,,
[Fras. Sydney] Highmes[2]	49	10	0	,,
[Ric.] Munden[3]	49	10	0	,,
[And.] Windsor[4]	49	10	0	,,
[Fras.] Godfrey[5]	49	10	0	,,
[Phil. Dormer,[6] K.]				
[Jno.] Lord Mordaunt,[7] W.	99	0	0	,,
Jas. Dormer,[8] W.	99	0	0	,,
[Henry Blount,[9] K.]				

CAPT.-LIEUT.

| Tho. Ferrers,[10] W. | 47 | 0 | 0 | ,, |

LIEUTENANTS.

Henry Browne[11]	23	10	0	,,
Jno. Pickering[12]	23	10	0	,,
Wm. Barrell[13]	23	10	0	,,
Ant. Hastings[14]	23	10	0	,,
[Gilbert] Nicholetts[15]	23	10	0	,,
[Jas.] Howard[16]	23	10	0	,,
Jno. Jefferson[17]	23	10	0	,,
[Mat.] Adams[18]	23	10	0	,,
[Ant.] *Pujolas*	23	10	0	,,
[Wm. West,[19] K.]				
Jno. Pocock,[20] W.	47	0	0	,,
[Walter Raleigh,[21] K.]				

ENSIGNS.

Maurice [Nassau] Zuylestein[22]	17	10	0	,,
Geoffrey De Culant[23]	17	10	0	,,
Gra[nada] Chester[24]	17	10	0	,,
Phil. Bragg[25]	17	10	0	,,
Jno. West[26]	17	10	0	,,
St. Denis Pujolas[27]	17	10	0	,,
Geo. Smith[28]	17	10	0	,,
Robt. Rich,[29] W.	33	0	0	,,
Val. Reeves,[30] W.	33	0	0	,,
Rowld. Campion,[31] W.	33	0	0	,,
[Ric. Pierson,[32] W.]				

	ADJT.	£	s.	d.	
Wm. Barrell [33]	- - - -	12	0	0	Bounty.
	QR.-MASTER.				
[Jno. Bibby,[34] K.]	- - -				
	SURGEON.				
Archdale Harris [35]	- - -	12	0	0	,,
	SURGEON'S MATE.				
Wm. Scott [36]	- - - -	7	10	0	,,

* The non-commissioned officers and privates who received bounty money were 38 sergeants, each of whom received £2 2s. 6d.; 38 corporals, each of whom received £1 12s. 6d., and 477 privates (including drummers), each of whom received £1 2s. 6d. At Schellenberg 7 sergts. were killed and 8 wounded; 75 privates were killed and 127 wounded.

[1] Third son of Sir Archibald Primrose, Bt., a Lord of Session. Appointed Lieut. in the King's Foot Guards 1 Sept. 1680. Adjt. 19 March 1686. Capt. and Lt.-Col. 21 March 1692. Bt.-Col. 1 March 1703. Wounded at Schellenberg where he commanded the Battalion. Promoted 2nd Major of the Guards 24 March 1705. Brigdr.-Gen. 1 Jan. 1707. Colonel of the Regt. now known as the 24th Foot 9 March 1708. Maj.-Gen. 1 Jan. 1710. Retd. from the Army in 1717. D. in 1731.

[2] Appointed Ens. in above Regt. 17 Apr. 1691. Capt. 1 Dec. 1693. Served at Ramillies and Malplaquet. Called "Francis Sydney" in the Army List for 1709. Sold his Comn. 1 June 1710.

[3] Son of Sir Ric. Munden, Knt. Appointed Capt. and Lt.-Col. in above Regt. 22 Apr. 1702. Served at Ramillies. Lt.-Col. of Lord Lovelace's newly-raised Regt. of Foot 12 Apr. 1706. Brigdr.-Gen. 12 Feb. 1712. Col. of Lord Lovelace's late Regt. in 1708. Appointed Colonel of a newly raised Regt. of Dragoons (now 13th Hussars) in 1715. Held this command until Nov. 1722.

[4] Appointed Cornet in the Rl. Regt. of Horse Guards 20 Feb. 1698. Capt. in the 1st Foot Guards 15 Jan. 1702. Bt.-Col. 1 Jan. 1706. Served at Ramillies. Wounded at Malplaquet. Col. of the Regt. now known as the 28th Foot 1 Oct. 1709. Brigdr.-Gen. 12 Feb. 1711. Held this command until Nov. 1715.

[5] Son of Colonel Chas. Godfrey, Master of the Jewel House, by his wife Arabella Churchill, sister of the Duke of Marlborough. Appointed Capt. and Lt.-Col. in the 1st Foot Guards 3 March 1703. Col. of the Regt. now known as the 16th Foot 25 March 1705. Groom of the bedchamber to Prince George of Denmark in 1706. Brigdr.-Gen. 1 Jan. 1710. Inherited half the real and personal estate of his uncle, Admiral George Churchill, who d. 8 May 1710. Sold his Colonelcy in 1711. D. 6 Oct. 1712.

[6] Appointed Lieut. and Capt. in the 1st Foot Guards 2 July 1700. Capt. and Lt.-Col. before 1704. Commanded the Battalion of Guards at Blenheim and gloriously fell at the head of his men.

[7] Eldest son of the celebrated Earl of Peterborough. Appointed Capt. and Lt.-Col. in above Regt. 30 Nov. 1703. Led the stormers at Schellenberg, where most of his grenadiers were killed. Lost his left arm at Blenheim. Appointed Colonel of the Rl. Scots Fusiliers 25 Aug. 1704. Transferred to 28th Foot 29 June 1706. Reappointed Colonel of the Rl. Scots Fusiliers 4 Sept. 1709. Brigdr.-Gen. 1 Jan. 1710. D. of the smallpox in Apr. 1710, leaving a son, Charles, who eventually succeeded as Earl of Peterborough.

[8] Son of Robert Dormer of Dorton, Bucks, by his 2nd wife. Appointed Lieut. and Capt. in above Regt. 1 May 1702. Capt. and Lt.-Col. 4 Apr. 1704. Served at Ramillies. Bt.-Col. 1 Jan. 1707. Appointed Col. of Lord Mohun's late Regt. of Foot 1 May 1708. Embarked for Spain in 1709. Distinguished himself at the battle of Saragossa. Present at the taking of Madrid. Taken prisoner with his Regt. at Brihuega in 1710. Brigdr.-Gen. 12 Feb. 1711. Raised a Regt. of Dragoons (now 14th Hussars) in 1715 and was appointed Colonel of the same. Served at the battle of Preston as a Brigdr.-Gen. Transferred to the Colonelcy of the 6th Foot 9 Apr. 1720. Maj.-Gen. 14 March 1727. Envoy to Portugal same year. Lt.-Gen. 4 Nov. 1735. Col. of the 1st Tp. of Horse Grendr. Guards 10 Feb. 1738. D. 24 Dec. 1741.

[9] Appointed Capt. and Lt.-Col. in above Regt. 6 March 1703. Killed at Schellenberg.

[10] Appointed Ens. in the 1st Foot Guards 24 Jan. 1692. Lieut. and Capt. 29 Apr. 1695. Capt.-Lieut. and Lt.-Col. 15 Feb. 1702. Wounded at Schellenberg. Capt. and Lt.-Col. 25 Aug. 1704. Bt.-Col. 25 Feb. 1705. Served at Ramillies and Malplaquet. Brigdr.-Gen. 1 Jan. 1710. Comns. renewed by George I.

[11] Appointed Lieut. and Capt. in above Regt. 13 June 1700. Served at Ramillies and Malplaquet. Qr.-Mr. 11 Jan. 1715.

[12] Appointed Ens. in above Regt. 1 Apr. 1689. Wounded at Steinkirk. Lieut. and Capt. 2 Aug. 1692. Out of the Regt. in March 1708.

[13] Appointed Lieut. and Capt. in above Regt. 27 March 1698. 1st Lieut. of Grendrs. in 1702. Capt. and Lt.-Col. 5 Jan. 1705. Bt.-Col. 1 Jan. 1707. Served throughout Marlborough's campaigns. Col. of the Regt. now known as the 28th Foot 27 Sept. 1715. Brigdr.-Gen. 7 March 1727. Transferred to the 22nd Foot 25 Aug. 1730. Col. of the 4th Foot 8 Aug. 1734. Maj.-Gen. 1 Nov. 1735. Lt.-Gen. 2 July 1739. Gov. of Pendennis Castle. D. 8 Aug. 1749. Bd. in Westminster Abbey. M.I.

[14] Appointed Lieut. and Capt. in above Regt. 8 June 1692. Served throughout Marlborough's campaigns. Out of the Regt. in 1715.

[15] Son of Gilbert Nicholetts by Mary, dau. of Edward Cornwall, of Mochas, Hereford. Ensign's Comn. not forthcoming. Appointed 2nd Lieut. to the Grendr. Cy. 15 March 1705. Adjt. 5 Apr. 1704. Capt.-Lieut. 24 March 1709. Served at Malplaquet. Out of the Regt. in 1715.

[16] Appointed Ens. in above Regt. 22 July 1693. Capt.-Lieut. and Qr.-Mr. of Col. Tho. Farrington's newly raised Regt. of Foot 16 Feb. 1694. Capt. 12 Sept. 1694. Placed on half-pay 28 Feb. 1698. Appointed Lieut. and Capt. in 1st Foot Guards 10 March 1702. Major of Col. Tho. Handasyde's Regt. of Foot (22nd Foot) in the West Indies in 1705. Lt.-Col. of last-named Regt. — Aug. 1715.

[17] Called "Jeffreyson" in some Lists. Appointed Ens. in the Rl. Regt. of Foot 26 Oct. 1701. Lieut. and Capt. in 1st Foot Guards 2 Apr. 1704. Out of the Regt. in 1708.

[18] Appointed Lieut. in above Regt. 1 May 1689. 1st Lieut. of Grendrs. in 1702. Appears among the officers who were wounded at Schellenberg in Hamilton's *Hist. of the Grenadier Guards*. Out of the Regt. 8 July 1705. On the half-pay List as Capt. of Foot in 1714.

[19] Appointed Ens. in above Regt. 1 Dec. 1693. 2nd Lieut. of the Grendr. Cy., with rank of Captain, 25 Oct. 1700. Killed at Schellenberg.

[20] Appointed Ens. in Brigdr.-Gen. Ingoldsby's Regt. of Foot 6 Feb. 1696. Lieut. and Capt. in the 1st Foot Guards 18 May 1702. Capt.-Lieut. 25 Aug. 1704. Served at Ramillies. Capt. 23 Dec. 1706. Bt.-Col. 1 Jan. 1707. Col. of a Regt. of Foot (aftds. disbanded) 15 June 1710. Col. of the Regt. now known as the 36th Foot 2 Dec. 1720. Col. of the Regt. now known as the 8th Foot 21 Apr. 1721. Brigdr.-Gen. 5 March 1727. D. in Apr. 1732.

[21] Appointed Ens. in above Regt. 2 June 1690. Lieut. and Capt. 22 June 1692. Killed at Schellenberg.

[22] Kinsman to Maj.-Gen. the Earl of Rochford. Generally called Count Maurice Nassau. Appointed Ens. to the Queen's Cy. in above Regt. 10 March 1702. Capt. in Brigdr.-Gen. Wm. Tatton's Regt. of Foot 25 Aug. 1704. Served at Ramillies. Lt.-Col. *en second* of Visct. Mountjoy's Regt. of Foot 5 March 1708. Lt.-Col. of Col. Wm. Watkins's Regt. of Foot 16 March 1709. Col. of a Regt. of Foot 12 Dec. 1711. Last-named Regt. was disbanded 12 Nov. 1712. Col. of a newly-raised Regt. in 1715. D. in 1722.

[23] Appointed Ens. in above Regt. 19 Apr. 1697. Serving in Flanders in 1709 as 2nd Lieut. of Grendrs. in same Regt. Out of the Army in 1715.

[24] Appointed Ens. in above Regt. 1 Apr. 1703. Cornet in the Duke of Schomberg's Regt. of Horse 24 Aug. 1705. Serving in Flanders in 1709.

[25] Appointed Ens. in above Regt. 10 March 1702. Capt. in Brigdr.-Gen. Tatton's Regt. of Foot 25 Aug. 1704. Lt.-Col. of the Earl of Isla's Regt. of Foot 6 May 1709. Colonel of the Regt. now known as the 28th Foot 10 Oct. 1734. Master of the Rl. Hospital at Kilmainham 1733–1735. Brigdr.-Gen. 18 Feb. 1742. Maj.-Gen. 5 July 1743. Served at Fontenoy. Lt.-Gen. 10 Aug. 1747. D. in 1759.

[26] Appointed Ens. in above Regt. 17 Oct. 1694. Out of the Regt. in 1705. Appointed Major of Col. Tho. Stanwix's newly-raised Regt. of Foot 12 Apr. 1706.

[27] Appointed Ens. in above Regt. 11 May 1694. Wounded at the siege of Namur 18 July 1695. Lieut. and Capt. 25 Aug. 1704. Served at Malplaquet. Out of the Regt. in 1715.

[28] Appointed Ens. in above Regt. 1 Oct. 1695. Lieut. and Capt. 25 Aug. 1704. Amongst the officers wounded at Schellenberg in Hamilton's *Hist. of the Grenadier Guards*. Served throughout Marlborough's campaigns. Comn. renewed by George I.

[29] Of Rosehall, Suffolk. Succeeded his bro. Charles as 4th Bart. Appointed Ens. in above Regt. 10 June 1700. Wounded at Schellenberg as well as at Blenheim. Capt. in Brigdr.-Gen. Wm. Tatton's Regt. of Foot 25 Aug. 1704. Transferred as Capt. to 1st Foot Guards 9 March 1708. Bt.-Col. 24 Aug. 1709. Appointed Col. of a Regt. of Foot (late Watkins's) 1 Jan. 1710. Was taken prisoner with other officers going to Gibraltar by the capture of the "Hunter" frigate off Cadiz by 3 French privateers (Letter from Tho. Leffever to Lord Dartmouth from Lisbon 13 Oct. 1710). Col. of the Regt. known as the 13th Hussars 19 Nov. 1722. Transferred to 8th Hussars 23 Sept. 1725. Col. of the 4th Hussars 13 May 1735. Brigdr.-Gen. 20 March 1727. Maj.-Gen. 12 Nov. 1735. Lieut.-Gen. 2 July 1739. Field-Marshal 28 Nov. 1757. Was an M.P. and Gov. of Chelsea Hospital. D. 1 Feb. 1768. By his will, dated 31 Oct. 1767, he desired to be buried in the vaults of St. George's, Hanover Square.

[30] Appointed Ens. in above Regt. 17 March 1699. Capt. in the Rl. Welsh Fusiliers 25 Aug. 1704. Out of last-named Regt. 24 Nov. 1708.

[31] Appointed Ens. in above Regt. 1 Apr. 1703 at the age of 13. Quitted the service soon after Blenheim, but rejoined the Army as Capt.-Lieut. of Lord Tunbridge's Regt. of Foot 12 Apr. 1706.

[32] This officer's name has been omitted in the MS. Appointed Ens. in above Regt. 10 March 1702. Wounded at Schellenberg (*Records*). Lieut. and Capt. 22 June 1709. Served throughout Marlborough's campaigns. Capt. in the Rl. Fusiliers 30 March 1711. Comn. renewed by George I. Capt. and Lt.-Col. in 1st Foot Guards 3 April 1718. Retd. 22 April 1742. D. 3 Jan. 1743, at York, and left directions that his body should lie in state 40 days! *Gentleman's Mag.*

[33] See note 13.

[34] Appointed Qr.-Mr. in above Regt. 13 June 1700. Killed at Schellenberg.

[35] Erroneously called "Archibald Harris" in some Lists. Appointed Surgeon to above Regt. 27 Dec. 1690. Served throughout Marlborough's campaigns. Comn. renewed by George I. D. in Apr. 1738. *Gent's Mag.*

[36] Appointed Surgeon to Col. Nich. Lepell's Regt. of Foot about 1705. Placed on half-pay in 1712.

THE ROYAL REGT. OF FOOT.*

1st Batt.

COLONEL.

	£	s.	d.	
[Geo.] Earl of Orkney	72	0	0	Bounty.

LIEUT-COLONEL COMMANDING.

[Jno. White,[1] K.]

CAPTAINS.

	£	s.	d.	
[Robt.] Kerr [2]	30	0	0	,,
[Geo.] Brown [3]	30	0	0	,,
[Alex.] Ross [4]	30	0	0	,,
[Archd.] Hamilton [5]	30	0	0	,,
[Jas.] Hume [6]	30	0	0	,,
[Ric.] Molesworth [7]	30	0	0	,,
[Chas.] Cockburn,[8] W.	60	0	0	,,
[Jas.] Cuningham,[9] W.	60	0	0	,,
[Alex.] Irwin, W.	60	0	0	,,
[Jas.] Abercrombie, W.	60	0	0	,,
[Jno. Murray,[10] K.]				

CAPT.-LIEUT.

	£	s.	d.	
Geo. Ogilvie [11]	14	0	0	,,

LIEUTENANTS.

	£	s.	d.	
Jas. Black [12]	14	0	0	,,
Jno. Seymour [13]	14	0	0	,,
[Alex.] Gordon [14]	14	0	0	,,
[Archd.] Colville [15]	14	0	0	,,
[And.] Kidd,[16] W.	28	0	0	,,
[Jas.] Ballantine,[17] W.	28	0	0	,,
[Alex.] White,[18] W.	28	0	0	,,
[Robt.] Straiton,[19] W.	28	0	0	,,
[Wm. Moor,[20] W.]				

ENSIGNS.

	£	s.	d.	
Jno. Murray [21]	11	0	0	,,
Jas. Bisset [22]	11	0	0	,,
J——- Wauchope [23]	11	0	0	,,
Jas. Stewart [24]	11	0	0	,,
Jas. White [25]	11	0	0	,,
[Alex.] Hume,[26] W.	22	0	0	,,
[David] Cunningham,[27] W.	22	0	0	,,
[Pat.] Morinier ?,[28] W.	22	0	0	,,
[Peter] Stewart,[29] W.	22	0	0	!,,
[Jas. Craig,[30] K.]				
[—— McDougal,[31] K.]				
[—— McIlroy,[32] K.]				

CHAPLAIN.

	£	s.	d.	
Saml. Noyes [33]	20	0	0	,,

ADJT.

	£	s.	d.	
Archd. Hamilton [34]	12	0	0	,,

S 8623.

THE BLENHEIM ROLL.

QUARTER-MASTER.

	£	s.	d.	
Wm. Weir 35 - - - - -	14	0	0	Bounty.

SURGEON.

| Peter Boullay 36 - - - - | 12 | 0 | 0 | ,, |

SURGEON'S MATES.

| J—— Ligas 37 - - - - | 7 | 10 | 0 | ,, |
| S[aml.] Demonty 38 - - - | 7 | 10 | 0 | ,, |

DRUM-MAJOR.

| J——- Bodil 39 - - - - | 6 | 0 | 0 | ,, |

PIPER.

| Adriel Duran 40 - - - - | 3 | 0 | 0 | ,, |

* The Royal Scots Regt. of Foot. The non-commissioned officers and men who received bounty-money were 27 sergeants, each of whom received £2; 32 corporals, each of whom received £1 10s.; 542 privates (including drummers), each of whom received £1. At Schellenberg the above battalion had 1 sergeant and 38 rank and file killed, and 3 sergeants and 103 rank and file wounded. *Records.*

¹ Served at Tangiers as a Captain in above Regt. in the reign of Charles II. Served at Steinkirk. Major 1 Aug. 1692. Lt.-Col. 31 Aug. same year. Bt.-Col. 1 March 1703. Severely wounded at Schellenberg. Killed at Blenheim. Bounty of £102 to his widow and 2 children.

² Called "Carr" in the MS. Appointed 2nd Lieut. in above Regt. in the reign of Charles II. 1st Lieut. in the reign of James II. Capt.-Lieut. 31 Dec. 1688. Capt. 1 Oct. 1689. Served several campaigns in Flanders under Wm. III. Bt.-Lt.-Col. 1 Jan. 1706. Served throughout Marlborough's campaigns. Comn. renewed by George I.

³ Appointed Ens. in above Regt. 1 Oct. 1689. Lieut. 1 Aug. 1692. Wounded at Landen. Bt.-Capt. 25 Aug. 1703. Capt. 3 May 1704. Served throughout Marlborough's campaigns. Comn. renewed by George I.

⁴ Appointed Capt. in above Regt. 2 May 1704. Served at Ramillies and Malplaquet. Out of the Regt. in 1715.

⁵ Appointed 2nd Lieut. of Grendrs. in above Regt. 10 May 1693. Wounded at the siege of Namur 23 July 1695, and again on 20 Aug. same year when storming the Terra Nova. Capt. 23 June 1704. Served in several of Marlborough's campaigns. Appointed a Brigade-Major in Spain 3 March 1711.

⁶ Erroneously called "Horne" in some of the Comn. Entry Books. Appointed Ens. in above Regt. 1 Oct. 1689. Capt.-Lieut. 1 June 1695. Capt. 1 Aug. 1695. Served at the siege of Namur. Among the officers wounded at Schellenberg in the *Records* of above Regt. Served throughout Marlborough's campaigns. Bt.-Major 1 Jan 1712. Lt.-Col. of above Regt. 1 July 1737. D. about 1742.

⁷ 2nd son of the 1st Visct. Molesworth. Was designed for the law, and sent to finish his studies at the Temple, but preferring a more active life, he went to Flanders and served as a Volunteer. The Earl of Orkney, his father's friend, procured an Ensigncy in the above Regt. for young Molesworth, and his Comn. was dated 14 Apr. 1702. Lieut's. Comn. not forthcoming. He brilliantly distinguished himself at the battle of Ramillies, where he acted as A.D.C. to Marlborough, and saved the Duke's life at the risk of his own. Capt. and Lt.-Col. in the Coldstream Guards 5 May 1705. Continued on Marlborough's staff, and was present at the relief of Brussels in 1708, and at the battle of Malplaquet in 1709. Appointed Col. of Col. Moor's late Regt. of Foot 9 July 1710. Col. of a newly-raised Regt. of Dragoons in 1715. Wounded at the battle of Preston, where he behaved with great bravery. M.P. for Swordes. Succeeded his bro. John as 3rd Viscount in 1726. Major-Gen. 18 Nov. 1735. Lt.-Gen. 2 July 1739. Gen. of Horse 28 Dec. 1746. Field-Marshal 19 Nov. 1757. Was Master-Gen. of the Irish Ordnance, and Commander-in-Chief of the Army in Ireland. D. 13 Oct. 1758.

⁸ Appointed 2nd Lieut. of the Grendr. Cy. in Col. Robt. Hodges's Regt. of Foot 31 Dec. 1688. Capt.-Lieut. 14 March 1689. Capt. of the Grendr. Cy. 1 Jan. 1692. Served at Landen. Transferred to the Grendr. Cy. in Rl. Scots Regt. of Foot 8 Mar. 1694. Bt.-Major 1 March 1703. Wounded at Schellenberg. Bt.-Lt.-Col. 1 Jan. 1706. Bt.-Col. 1 March 1711. Served throughout Marlborough's campaigns. Appointed 2nd Lt.-Col. of the Rl. Scots in 1711. Brigdr.-Gen. in 1735. "Died in King St., St. James's, suddenly, on 21 July 1738, after eating cucumbers and drinking cyder." *Gent's. Mag.* 1738.

⁹ Appointed Capt. in above Regt. 8 March 1694. Bt.-Major 1 Jan. 1706. Served throughout Marlborough's campaigns. Bt.-Lt.-Col. 1 Jan. 1712. Appointed 2nd Major of the Royal Scots before 1715. Attained the rank of Colonel, and at the time of his death in 1738 was Lieut.-Govr. of Fort George in Scotland.

¹⁰ Appointed Capt. in the Rl. Regt. of Foot 1 May 1688. Killed at Schellenberg. Bounty of £60 to his widow and child.

[11] Appointed Qr.-Mr. and Marshal to the Royal Regt. of Foot 16 Apr. 1683. Lieut. 1 Jan. 1690. Capt.-Lieut. 3 Aug. 1704. Served at Ramillies and Malplaquet. Out of the Regt. in 1715.

[12] Appointed Lieut. in above Regt. 12 Apr. 1691. Wounded at Landen. Out of the Regt. in 1708.

[13] Appointed Lieut. in above Regt. 14 Apr. 1702. Served throughout Marlborough's campaigns. Comn. renewed by George I.

[14] Appointed Ens. in above Regt. 29 May 1696. Lieut. 3 March 1703. Served throughout Marlborough's campaigns. Capt. and Bt.-Major in May 1710. Placed on half-pay in 1713. Lt.-Col. 28 Feb. 1723. Serving in the 41st Foot in 1742.

[15] Appointed Lieut. in above Regt. 2 Aug. 1695. Served throughout Marlborough's campaigns. Comn. renewed by George I. Capt.-Lieut. 8 Feb. 1736. Capt. 10 July 1736. Out of the Regt. 24 Aug. 1738.

[16] Appointed Lieut. in above Regt. 1 Nov. 1691. Wounded at Schellenberg. Not in any subsequent List.

[17] Appointed Ens. in above Regt. 1 May 1692. Lieut. 28 May 1696. Wounded at Schellenberg. Capt. 1 Nov. 1708. Served throughout Marlborough's campaigns. Comn. renewed by George I.

[18] Appointed Ens. in above Regt. 10 May 1693. Lieut. 23 June 1704. Lost a leg at Schellenberg. Continued on full pay until Feb. 1710, when Marlborough recommended that this officer should be made a "Poor Knight of Windsor" by Queen Anne. *Dispatches*, Vol. IV., p. 688.

[19] Appointed Ens. in above Regt. 10 May 1693. Lieut. 23 June 1704. Served throughout Marlborough's campaigns. Capt.-Lieut. before 1715.

[20] Appointed Lieut. in above Regt. 1 Aug. 1692. Wounded at Schellenberg and died of his wounds soon afterwards. His widow received £28 bounty.

[21] A certain John Murray was appointed Ens. in above Regt. 1 Aug. 1692. Out of the Regt. in 1703.

[22] Appointed Ens. in the above Regt. 22 May 1694. Out of the Regt. in 1708.

[23] Possibly meant for *Andrew* Wauchope, who was appointed 2nd Lieut. of the Grendr. Cy. in the 2nd Batt. of above Regt. 1 Dec. 1705, and served at Malplaquet.

[24] Ensign's Comn. not forthcoming. Out of the Regt. in 1708.

[25] Appointed Ens. in above Regt. 23 June 1704. Lieut. 2 Nov. 1708. Served throughout Marlborough's campaigns. Comn. renewed by George I.

[26] Appointed Ens. in above Regt. 23 June 1704. Lieut. 3 Apr. 1707. Out of the Regt. in 1715.

[27] Appointed Ens. in the above Regt. 12 Feb. 1702. Wounded at Schellenberg. Out of the Regt. in 1708.

[28] Called "Le Morimer" in former Lists. Appointed Ens. in Lord Murray's Regt. of Foot in Apr. 1694. Lieut. 14 Oct. 1696. Appointed Ens. in the Royal Scots 1 July 1702. Wounded at Schellenberg. Was recommended for a Cy. in the New Levies in 1706 by the Earl of Orkney. *War Office MS.*

[29] Ensign's Comn. not forthcoming. Wounded at Schellenberg. Lieut. 2 Apr. 1707. Served throughout Marlborough's campaigns. Comn. renewed by George I.

[30] Ensign's Comn. not forthcoming.

[31] and [32] Comns. not forthcoming. Killed at Schellenberg.

[33] Appointed Chaplain to above Regt. 1 Dec. 1692. Left the Regt. 25 March 1709.

[34] See note 5.

[35] Appointed Qr.-Mr. to the 1st Batt. of above Regt. 1 June 1697. Capt. 20 Sept. 1707. Served throughout Marlborough's campaigns. Comn. renewed by George I.

[36] This officer's name is spelt differently in every List in which the name occurs. He was appointed Surgeon to Col. Arch. Douglas's Regt. of Foot 18 Oct. 1688. Transferred to the Rl. Regt. of Foot in Dec. 1688. Served throughout Wm. III's. and Marlborough's campaigns. Left the Regt. before 1715.

[37] Untraced.

[38] Appointed Surgeon to Col. Owen Wynne's Regt. of Foot 25 March 1705. A certain Samu Demonty was placed on half pay as a Lieut. in Wynne's Regt. in 1713.

[39] and [40] Untraced.

THE ROYAL REGT. OF FOOT.*
2ND BATT.

MAJOR COMMANDING.

	£	s.	d.	
[And.] Hamilton [1]	45	0	0	Bounty.

CAPTAINS.

[Jno.] Bannerman [2]	30	0	0	,,
[Pat.] Gordon.	30	0	0	,,
[Robt.] Hamilton [3]	30	0	0	,,
[Wm.] Brisbane [4]	30	0	0	,,
[Tho.] Bruce,[5] W.	60	0	0	,,
[Wm.] Kerr,[6] W.	60	0	0	,,
[Jas.] Lindsay,[7] W.	60	0	0	,,
[Wm.] Montgomery,[8] W.	60	0	0	,,
[Wm.] Melville,[9] W.	60	0	0	,,
[Jno. Baily,[10] K.]				
[Lord Forbes,[11] K.]				

LIEUTENANTS.

[Jno.] Erskine [12]	14	0	0	,,
[Duncan] McKenzie [13]	14	0	0	,,
[Edwd] Murray [14]	14	0	0	,,
[Jas.] Graham [15]	14	0	0	,,
[Jas.] Dickson,[16] W.	28	0	0	,,
[Ben.] Pearson,[17] W.	28	0	0	,,
[Chas.] Harraway,[18] W.	28	0	0	,,
[Theod.] Hay,[19] W.	28	0	0	,,
[Alex.] Hamilton, [20] W.	28	0	0	,,
[Wm.] Vernall,[21] W.	28	0	0	,,
[Jno.] McQueen,[22] W.	28	0	0	,,
[Walter] Innes,[23] W.	28	0	0	,,
[Jas. Livingston,[24] K.]				
[Tho. Kerr,[25] K.]				

ENSIGNS.

[Wm.] Muirhead [26]	11	0	0	,,
[Jno.] Gordon [27]	11	0	0	,,
—— Elliot,[28] W.	22	0	0	,,
[Alex.] Inglis,[29] W.	22	0	0	,,
—— Murray,[30] W.	22	0	0	,,
[Geo.] Inglis,[31] W.	22	0	0	,,
[Jas.] Moor,[32] W.	22	0	0	,,
[Jas.] Straiton,[33] W.	22	0	0	,,
[Geo. McConway,[34] K.]				
[Wm. Lyall,[35] W.]				

ADJT.

[Wm.] Melville,[36]	12	0	0	,,

QUARTER-MASTER.

[Geo.] Hadden,[37] W.	28	0	0	,,

* The non-commissioned officers and men who received bounty money were 24 sergeants, each of whom received £2; 29 corporals, each of whom received £1 10s.; 487 privates (including drummers), each of whom received £1.

¹ Appointed Capt. in Lord Geo. Hamilton's Inniskilling Regt. of Foot in 1690 or 1691. Capt. in the Rl. Regt. of Foot 1 Aug. 1692. Major 20 July 1695. Bt.-Lt -Col. 1 March 1703. Regtal.-Lt.-Col. 3 Aug. 1704. Bt.-Col. 1 Jan. 1706. Served throughout the campaigns of Wm. III. Commanded above Batt. at the battle of Wynendale in 1708, and at Malplaquet in 1709. Returned to Ireland in June 1710 on private affairs (*Marlborough Dispatches*, Vol. V. p. 57). Sold his Lt.-Colonelcy 20 March 1711 to Sir Jas. Abercrombie, Bt.

² 2nd son of Alex. Bannerman, of Elsick, co. Kincardine. Appointed Ens. in above Regt. before 1680. Recommissioned 16 May 1684. 2nd Lieut. 1 Jan. 1685. Capt. 1 Oct. 1689. Is said to have served at Tangiers in Capt. Home's Cy. 1680–1683. Out of the Regt. in 1708. In Burke's *Baronetage* this officer is said to have been in James II.'s Guards.

³ Appointed Capt.-Lieut. of Col. Jno. Buchan's Regt. of Foot 16 Jan. 1692. Placed on half-pay in 1697. Appointed Capt. in the Rl. Regt. of Foot 26 Apr. 1698. Served throughout Marlborough's campaigns. Comn. renewed by George I.

⁴ Appointed Lieut. in above Regt. 10 May 1693. Capt. 4 May 1704. Served throughout Marlborough's campaigns. Comn. renewed by George I.

⁵ Appointed Ens. in above Regt. before 13 May 1684 when he was recommissioned. Lieut. 31 Dec. 1688. Capt. 1 Oct. 1689. Served throughout Wm. III.'s and Marlborough's campaigns. Out of the Regt. in 1715.

⁶ Appointed Capt. in above Regt. 8 March 1694. Bt.-Major 1 March 1703. Wounded at Schellenberg. Out of the Regt. in 1709.

⁷ The Hon. Jas. Lindsay, 2nd son of Wm., 2nd Earl of Lindsay. Appointed Ens. in above Regt. 10 May 1693. Capt. 3 Aug. 1697. Out of the Regt. in 1708. In Burke's *Extinct Peerage* this officer is stated to have been a "Colonel in the army, and to have been killed at Almanza."

⁸ 2nd son of Sir Jas. Montgomery, 2nd Bart., of Skelmorlie. Appointed Ens. in above Regt. 14 Apr. 1702. Capt. of Grendrs. 1 May 1704. Appointed Major of the 2nd Tp. of Horse Grendr. Guards 6 March 1708. Lt.-Col. of said Tp. 2 Sept. 1709. Out of the army 10 Feb. 1710.

⁹ Appointed Ens. in above Regt. 1 Oct. 1684. Lieut. 10 May 1693. Capt.'s Comn. not forthcoming. Served throughout Marlborough's campaigns. Comn. renewed by George I. D. in 1716.

¹⁰ Appointed Lieut. in above Regt. 14 Apr. 1702. Capt's. Comn. not forthcoming. D. of wounds received at Schellenberg. Bounty of £60 to his widow and children.

¹¹ Called "Arthur, Lord Forbes" in the *MS. Army List* for 1702. D. of wounds received at Blenheim.

¹² Appointed 1st Lieut. of Grendrs. in above Regt. 1 June 1695. Out of the Regt. in 1708.

¹³ Appointed Lieut. in above Regt. 1 June 1695. Out of the Regt. in 1708.

¹⁴ Appointed Lieut. in above Regt. 22 May 1691. Out of the Regt. in 1708.

¹⁵ Appointed Lieut. in above Regt. 12 Feb. 1702. Served throughout Marlborough's campaigns. Comn. renewed by George I.

¹⁶ Appointed Ens. in above Regt. 1 May 1692. Lieut. 2 March 1703. Wounded at Schellenberg and Malplaquet. Out of the Regt. in 1715.

¹⁷ Appointed Lieut. in above Regt. 1 Oct. 1689. Wounded at Schellenberg. Served at Oudenarde. Out of the Regt. in Nov. 1708.

¹⁸ Appointed Lieut. in above Regt. 22 May 1694. Served at Malplaquet. Out of the Regt. in 1715.

¹⁹ Appointed Lieut. in above Regt. 29 May 1696. Wounded at Schellenberg. Out of the Regt. in 1715.

²⁰ Appointed Ens. in above Regt. 1 June 1697. 1st Lieut. of Grendrs. 4 March 1703. Wounded at Schellenberg. Out of the Regt. in 1709.

²¹ Called "Jas. Vernall" in his first Comn. as Ens. in above Regt. 1 May 1692. Lieut. 1 Aug. 1695. Wounded at the siege of Namur. Wounded at Schellenberg. In his application for a Comn. in the New Levies in 1706, this officer states that he had been page to the Duke of Marlborough. Out of the Regt. in 1715.

²² Appointed Ens. in above Regt. 22 May 1694. Lieut. 23 June 1704. Served throughout Marlborough's campaigns. Capt. in 1716 *vice* Melville, deceased.

²³ Appointed Ens. in above Regt. 2 Aug. 1695. Served at the siege of Namur. Lieut. 24 June 1704. Served throughout Marlborough's campaigns. Comn. renewed by George I.

²⁴ Appointed Ens. in above Regt. 1 Aug. 1692. Lieut. 28 May 1696. Killed at Schellenberg. Probably son of Capt. Robt. Livingston, who fell at Steinkirk in 1692.

²⁵ Appointed Lieut. in above Regt. 16 July 1696. D. of wounds received at Schellenberg. Bounty of £28 to his widow and children.

²⁶ First Comn. not forthcoming. Capt. 1 June 1707. Out of the Regt. 3 Nov. 1708.

²⁷ Appointed Ens. in above Regt. 1 Aug. 1692. Out of the Regt. in 1708.

²⁸ First Comn. not forthcoming. Wounded at Schellenberg. Out of the Regt. in 1708.

[29] Appointed Ens. in above Regt. 10 May 1693. Wounded at Schellenberg. Out of the Regt. in 1708.

[30] Untraced.

[31] Appointed Ens. in above Regt. 28 May 1696. Lieut. 1 March 1703. 1st Lieut. of Grendrs. 1 Nov. 1708. Served throughout Marlborough's campaigns. Comn. renewed by George I.

[32] Appointed Ens. in above Regt. 23 June 1704. Wounded at Schellenberg. Out of the Regt. 26 May 1708. Possibly killed at Oudenarde.

[33] First Comn. not forthcoming. Wounded at Schellenberg. Lieut. 25 March 1705. Served throughout Marlborough's campaigns. Comn. renewed by George I.

[34] Appointed Ens. in above Regt. 16 July 1696.

[35] Appointed Ens. in above Regt. 28 May 1696. D. of wounds received at Blenheim.

[36] See note 9.

[37] Comn. as Qr.-Mr. not forthcoming. Appointed Lieut. in above Regt. 1 June 1706. Resigned his post of Quarter-Master about same date. Served at Malplaquet. Out of the Regt. in 1715.

GENERAL CHURCHILL'S REGT. OF FOOT.*

COLONEL.

	£	s.	d.	
Chas. Churchill - - - -	72	0	0	Bounty.

LIEUT.-COLONEL COMMANDING.

| Henry Peyton,[1] W. - - - | 102 | 0 | 0 | ,, |

MAJOR.

CAPTAINS.

Jno. Hetley,[2] W. - - - -	60	0	0	,,
[Oliver Luke,[3] K.] - - -				
Jno. Meoles,[4] W. - - - -	60	0	0	,,
Jno. Slaughter,[5] W. - - -	60	0	0	,,
Wm. Lloyd - - - -	30	0	0	,,
Chas. Churchill - - - -	30	0	0	,,
Jno. Chivers[6] - - - -	30	0	0	,,
[*Hen.*] *Disney* - - - -	30	0	0	,,

CAPT.-LIEUT.

| Ric. Abington[7] - - - - | 14 | 0 | 0 | ,, |

LIEUTENANTS.

Jno. Melville[8] - - - -	14	0	0	,,
Jno. Preston[9] - - - -	14	0	0	,,
[Geo. Palfrey,[10] K.] - - -				
[Alex. Scrimshire,[11] K.] - - -				
Tho. Pyne[12] - - - -	14	0	0	,,
Hugh Scott[13] - - - -	14	0	0	,,
Tho. White[14] - - - -	14	0	0	,,
Jno. Scott[15] - - - -	14	0	0	,,
Wm. Kenny[16] - - - -	14	0	0	,,
Jno. Grierson[17] - - - -	14	0	0	,,
Nat. Gittings[18] - - - -	14	0	0	,,

ENSIGNS.

Peter Grant[19] - - - -	11	0	0	,,
Robt. Melville[20] - - - -	11	0	0	,,
Tho. Smith,[21] W. - - -	22	0	0	,,
Hugh Montgomery,[22] W. - - -	22	0	0	,,
[Jas.] Bolton,[23] W. - - -	22	0	0	,,
—— Campion,[24] W. - - -	22	0	0	,,
[Tho. Harrison,[25] K.] - - -				
[—— Caldicot,[26] K.] - - -				

CHAPLAIN.

| Jno. Sandby[27] - - - - | 20 | 0 | 0 | ,, |

ADJT.

[Alex. Scrimshire,[28] K.] - -

THE BLENHEIM ROLL.

QR.-MR.

£ s. d.

Owen Evans ²⁹ - - - - 14 0 0 Bounty.

SURGEON.

Jno. Smallbones ³⁰ - - - 12 0 0 „

SURGEON'S MATE.

[Alex. Arthur] ³¹ - - - - 7 10 0 „

* The 3rd Buffs. The non-commissioned officers and men who received bounty money were 34 sergeants, each of whom received £2; 34 corporals, each of whom received £1 10s.; 491 privates (including drummers), each of whom received £1. At Schellenberg this Regt. had 2 officers and 3 men killed and 37 men wounded.

¹ 3rd son of Dr. Algernon Peyton, of Doddington, in the Isle of Ely. Appointed Lieut. in above Regt. (then called the "Holland Regt.") 19 July 1683. Capt. 23 Oct. 1685. Major 1 Jan. 1691. Lt.-Col. 26 Feb. 1694. Bt.-Col. 1 March 1703. Brigdr.-Gen. 12 Feb. 1711. Served all through the wars of Wm. III. and Queen Anne. D. in 1724.

² Appointed 2nd Lieut. in the composite Battalion of Foot sent to Virginia in 1676. Ens. in 1st Foot Guards 18 Aug. 1676. Lieut. 1 May 1680. Capt.'s Comn. in Prince Geo. of Denmark's Regt. of Foot 31 Dec. 1688 (*Flanders Army List* for 1694). Bt.-Major 1 Jan. 1704. Out of the Regt. 1 Jan. 1708.

³ Appointed Ens. in the Holland Regt. 1 March 1681. Lieut. 26 Sept. 1688. Capt. 1 Feb. 1690. Taken prisoner by the French near Fleurus 20 June 1692. Served several campaigns under Wm. III. D. of wounds received at Blenheim.

⁴ Appointed Ens. in above Regt. 1 Sept. 1679. Lieut. 1 Nov. 1685. Capt. 20 Feb. 1689. Served several campaigns under Wm. III. and Marlborough. Left the Regt. 2 Jan. 1708.

⁵ Appointed Capt. in above Regt. 18 May 1702. Bt.-Lt.-Col. 1 Jan. 1708. Out of the Regt. in 1715.

⁶ Called "Thos. Chivers" in the *Flanders Army List* for 1709. Bt.-Major 1 Jan. 1708. Out of the Regt. in 1715.

⁷ Appointed Lieut. in above Regt. 1 Apr. 1690. Capt.-Lieut. 24 Nov. 1702. Capt. 25 Aug. 1704. Served several campaigns under Wm. III. and Marlborough. Out of the Regt. 24 May 1709.

⁸ Appointed 2nd Lieut. of Grendrs. 1 May 1692. Bt.-Capt. 1 May 1708. Capt.-Lieut. 24 May 1709. Killed at Malplaquet.

⁹ Appointed Lieut. in above Regt. 14 Sept. 1693. Served throughout Marlborough's campaigns. Comn. renewed by George I. D. in 1716.

¹⁰ Appointed Lieut. in above Regt. 12 Feb. 1702. Bounty of £28 to his widow.

¹¹ Called "Scrimsour" in one List. Appointed Lieut. in above Regt. 1 Jan. 1690. Adjt. 18 May 1702.

¹² Appointed Lieut. in above Regt. 7 May 1694. Served at Malplaquet. Out of the Regt. in 1715.

¹³ Appointed 1st Lieut. of Grendrs. in above Regt. 20 May 1689. Bt.-Capt. 1 May 1708. Capt.-Lieut. 9 Aug. 1708. Capt. 24 May 1709. Killed at Malplaquet. From 1698 to 1701 this officer was quartered at the Hull blockhouse, and in the Drypool registers is still to be seen occasional mention of "Hugh Scott, gentleman officer in the Barwick [barrack]."

¹⁴ Appointed Ens. in above Regt. 1 Oct. 1697. 2nd Lieut. of the Grendr. Cy. 15 Apr. 1703. Served at Malplaquet as 1st Lieut. of the Grendr. Cy. Out of the Regt. in 1715.

¹⁵ Appointed Lieut. in above Regt. 29 July 1703. Out of the Regt. in 1708.

¹⁶ Appointed Ens. in above Regt. 1 May 1692. Lieut. 24 Oct. 1694. Out of the Regt. in 1708.

¹⁷ Called "Grearson" in the MS. Appointed Ens. 1 Jan. 1692. Adjt. 14 Sept. 1693. Lieut. 1 Sept. 1697. Resigned the Adjutancy in 1702. Reappointed Adjt. 25 Aug. 1704. Bt.-Capt. 1 May 1708. Served throughout Marlborough's campaigns. Wounded at Malplaquet. Regtal.-Capt. before 1 Jan. 1715.

¹⁸ Appointed Lieut. in above Regt. 1 Aug. 1689. Served in Wm. III.'s campaigns. Capt.-Lieut. 25 Aug. 1704. Bt.-Capt. 1 May 1708. Capt. 9 Aug. 1708. Served throughout Marlborough's campaigns. Comn. renewed by George I.

¹⁹ Appointed Ens. in above Regt. 1 Oct. 1697. Lieut. 25 Jan. 1705. Out of the Regt. 20 Apr. 1708.

²⁰ Appointed Ens. in above Regt. 15 July 1704. Lieut. 9 Aug. 1708. Served throughout Marlborough's campaigns. Comn. renewed by George I.

²¹ Comn. as Ens. not forthcoming. Out of the Regt. in 1708.

²² Appointed Ens. in above Regt. 14 Sept. 1693. Lieut. 25 Aug. 1704. Served throughout Marlborough's campaigns. Wounded at Malplaquet. Capt. before 1715.

²³ Appointed Ens. in above Regt. 14 Sept. 1693. Lieut. 25 Aug. 1704. Served throughout Marlborough's campaigns. Capt. 24 Aug. 1715.

²⁴ Comn. as Ens. not forthcoming. Not in any subsequent List of above Regt.

²⁵ Appointed Ens. in above Regt. 24 Nov. 1702. Killed at Schellenberg.

²⁶ Comn. as Ens. not forthcoming. Killed at Schellenberg.

²⁷ Appears to have been only acting Chaplain in 1704 as in the *Flanders Army List* for 1709, the date of his Comn. is given as 12 Aug. 1706. Was secretary to Gen. Churchill in Flanders, and was recommended for a prebendal stall in Worcester Cathedral by Marlborough in 1710.—*Marlborough Dispatches*.

²⁸ See note 11.

²⁹ Appointed Qr.-Mr. to above Regt. 14 Sept. 1693. Out of the Regt. in 1708.

³⁰ Appointed Surgeon to above Regt. 31 Dec. 1688. Physician to the Duke of Argyll in Spain 3 March 1711. Surgeon to Fort St. Anne in Minorca 20 Sept. 1712.

³¹ Name omitted in the MS. Served as Surgeon's Mate to above Regt. from 1694 (*Flanders Army List* for 1694). Appointed Surgeon to Col. Geo. Preston's Regt. of Foot (Cameronians) 28 July 1706. Comn. renewed by George I.

BRIGADIER-GENERAL WEBB'S REGT. OF FOOT.*

COLONEL.

	£	s.	d.	
[Jno. Richmond] Webb - - -	72	0	0	Bounty.

LIEUT.-COLONEL COMMANDING.

[Ric.] Sutton[1] - - - - -	51	0	0	,,

MAJOR.

[Lewis] Ramsay[2] - - - -	45	0	0	,,

CAPTAINS.

[Ant.] Colombière[3] - - - -	30	0	0	,,
Ralph Congreve[4] - - - -	30	0	0	,,
[Peter] Hammers[5] - - - -	30	0	0	,,
Wm. Congreve[6] - - - -	30	0	0	,,
[Fras.] Napier[7] - - - -	30	0	0	,,
[Edmund] Fielding[8] - - -	30	0	0	,,
[Jno.] Farcey[9] - - - -	30	0	0	,,
[Roger] Cator[10] - - - -	30	0	0	,,
[Leond. Lloyd,[11] W.] - -				

CAPT.-LIEUT.

Verney Lloyd[12] - - - -	14	0	0	,,

LIEUTENANTS.

──── Walker[13] - - - -	14	0	0	,,
[Peter] De Cosne[14] - - -	14	0	0	,,
[Jas.] Adams[15] - - - -	14	0	0	,,
[Peter] Ribton[16] - - - -	14	0	0	,,
[Jno.] Balfour[17] - - - -	14	0	0	,,
[Henry] Clavers[18] - - -	14	0	0	,,
[Jno.] Morton[19] - - - -	14	0	0	,,
[Joachim] Goudet[20] - - -	14	0	0	,,
[Henry] Whitney - - - -	14	0	0	,,
[Ben.] Cuttle[21] - - - -	14	0	0	,,
[Jno.] Bozier,[22] W. - - -	28	0	0	,,
[Wm.] Kerr or Carr[23] - -	14	0	0	,,

ENSIGNS.

[Bernard] Smith[24] - - -	11	0	0	,,
Paul Lewis[25] - - - -	11	0	0	,,
[Henry] Fletcher[26] - - -	11	0	0	,,
──── Barton[27] - - - -	11	0	0	,,
[Edwd.] Hobart[28] - - -	11	0	0	,,
[Chas.] Mason,[29] W. - -	22	0	0	,,
Leond. Lloyd,[30] W. - -	22	0	0	,,
[──── Savage (sic),[31] K.]				

CHAPLAIN.

Geo. Powell[32] - - - -	20	0	0	,,

ADJT.

Henry Whitney - - - -	12	0	0	,,

	QR.-MR.	£	s.	d.	
Ben. Cuttle [33]	- - - - -	14	0	0	Bounty.
	SURGEON.				
Jas. Chambers [34]	- - - -	12	0	0	,,
	SURGEON'S MATE.				
Chas. Lowndes [35]	- - - -	7	10	0	,,

* The 8th (King's) Regt. of Foot. The non-commissioned officers and men who received bounty money were 36 sergeants, each of whom received £2 ; 39 corporals, each of whom received £1 10s. ; 629 privates (including drummers), each of whom received £1. At Schellenberg there were 5 privates killed ; 2 sergeants and 31 privates wounded.

[1] 2nd son of Robt. Sutton, who was nephew of Robt. Sutton, created Viscount Lexinton by Charles I. Appointed Eus. in Visct. Castleton's Regt. of Foot 1 Apr. 1689. Capt. 1 June 1693. Major of Col. Richmond Webb's Regt. of Foot 14 Apr. 1701. Lt.-Col. 10 Sept. 1702. Bt.-Col. 2 Aug. 1704. Lt.-Govr. of Hull 11 May 1707. Col. of a Regt. of Foot (late Macartney's) 23 March 1709. Brigdr.-Gen. 1 Jan. 1710. M.P. for Newark same year. Govr. of Hull 20 July 1711. Col. of Brigdr.-Gen. Freake's Regt. (19th Foot) 3 Apr. 1712. C.-in-C. of the troops in garrison at Bruges 3 Oct. 1713. Served several campaigns under Wm. III. and Marlborough. D. a Lt.-Gen. in July 1737.

[2] Called "Louis de Ramsay" in the *Records of the 8th Foot*. Appointed Major of above Regt. 10 Dec. 1702. Bt.-Lt.-Col. 1 Jan. 1706. Regtal.-Lt.-Col. 23 March 1709. Killed at Malplaquet.

[3] Appointed 1st Lieut. of the Grendr. Cy. in above Regt. 12 Apr. 1689. Served in the Irish campaign. Capt. of Grendrs. 19 March 1691. Bt.-Major 25 Aug. 1704. Regtal.-Major 23 March 1709. Lt.-Col. *en second* to the Coldstream Guards 5 March 1708. Qr.-Mr.-Gen. of the Forces employed in Lt.-Gen. Erle's expedition by sea 6 July 1708. Bt.-Col. 1 March 1711. Regtal.-Lt.-Col. of 8th Foot before 1715. Served at Sheriffmuir. Sold his Lt.-Colonelcy in 1716.

[4] 2nd son of Jno. Congreve, of Congreve, co. Stafford. Appointed Ens. in above Regt. 21 March 1689. Capt.-Lieut. 15 Apr. 1692. Capt. 25 Feb. 1693. Appointed Lt.-Col. of Col. Wm. Breton's Regt. of Foot 25 March 1705. Taken prisoner at Almanza. Lt.-Gov. of Gibraltar 25 June 1713. Held this post until 1716.

[5] Called "Hamers" in the *Army List* for 1709. Appointed Capt.-Lieut. in above Regt. 25 Feb. 1693. Capt. 25 Apr. 1694. Cy. reduced in 1697. Reappointed Capt. 31 May 1701. Bt.-Major 1 Jan. 1707. Bt.-Lt.-Col. 1 Jan. 1712. Regtal.-Major before 1715. Served throughout Marlborough's campaigns. Killed at the battle of Sheriffmuir.

[6] Youngest son of Jno. Congreve, of Congreve, co. Stafford. Served in Col. Justin Macarthy's Regt. of Foot in Ireland previous to the Revolution. Capt. in Lord Danby's Volunteer Regt. of Dragoons 16 July 1690. Appointed Capt.-Lieut. of the Princess Anne of Denmark's Regt. of Foot 25 Apr. 1694. Capt. 30 May 1696. Bt.-Major 1 July 1706. Bt.-Lt.-Col. 1 Jan. 1712. Served throughout Marlborough's campaigns. Ancestor of Lt.-Gen. Wm. Congreve, R.A., who was created a Bart. in 1812.

[7] Called "Napper" in the MS. Appointed Ens. in above Regt. 8 June 1689. Lieut. 24 March 1691. Capt. of the Grendr. Cy. 25 Apr. 1694. Placed on half-pay in 1697. Reappointed Capt. 12 Feb. 1702. Out of the Regt. in 1708.

[8] Appointed Ens. in the 1st Foot Guards 15 Dec. 1696. Made Captain in Brigdr.-Gen. Webb's Regt. of Foot before 1704 (Comn. not forthcoming). Major of Lord Tunbridge's Regt. of Foot 12 Apr. 1706. Succeeded Col. Brazier in command of a Regt. of Foot about 1709. Placed on half-pay in 1713. Appointed Colonel of the Regt. now known as the 41st Foot 11 March 1719. D. in 1741 as a Lt.-Gen.

[9] Appointed Capt. in above Regt. 2 Apr. 1704. Served at Malplaquet. Comn. renewed by George I. Major 6 Apl. 1720. Serving in 1730.

[10] Appointed Ens. in above Regt. 20 Oct. 1696. Lieut.'s and Capt.'s Comns. not forthcoming. Out of the Regt. in 1706.

[11] This officer has been wrongly placed among the Ensigns in the *MS. Roll* at the Record Office. See note 30.

[12] Appointed Lieut. in above Regt. 25 Feb. 1696. Capt.-Lieut.'s Comn. not forthcoming. Out of the Regt. in 1708.

[13] Lieut.'s Comn. not forthcoming. Out of the Regt. in 1708.

[14] Appointed Ens. in above Regt. 9 Oct. 1689. Lieut. 30 Apr. 1694. Served at Malplaquet. Comn. renewed by George I. Retired in 1716.

[15] Appointed Ens. in above Regt. 30 Dec. 1693. Lieut. 31 May 1701. Out of the Regt. before 1706. A certain Jas. Adams was appointed Capt. in Col. Owen Wynne's Regt. of Foot 25 March 1705.

[16] First Comn. not forthcoming. Appointed Lieut. to the Lt.-Col.'s Cy. in above Regt. 25 Aug. 1704. Served at Malplaquet. Out of the Regt. in 1715.

[17] Appointed Lieut. in above Regt. 1 Aug. 1702. Capt. 4 May 1707. Qr.-Mr. before 1709. Served at Malplaquet.

[18] Appointed Lieut. in above Regt. 9 Oct. 1692. Out of the Regt. in 1708.

[19] Appointed Ens. in the above Regt. 14 Oct. 1695. 1st Lieut. of the Grendr. Cy. 10 Dec. 1702. Served at Malplaquet. Capt. before 1713, in which year his Cy. was reduced. On half-pay in 1714.

[20] Appointed Ens. in above Regt. 6 Dec. 1694. Lieut.'s Comn. not forthcoming. Capt.-Lieut. 16 May 1707. Served at Malplaquet. Comn. as Capt. renewed by George I. On half-pay in 1722.

[21] Appointed Ens. in above Regt. 2 Aug. 1689. Lieut. 15 Apr. 1692. Qr.-Mr. 1 Sept. 1697. Capt. 25 March 1705. Served throughout Marlborough's campaigns. Killed at the battle of Sheriffmuir.

[22] Appointed Lieut. in above Regt. 25 Aug. 1704. Wounded at Schellenberg and Blenheim. Served at Malplaquet.

[23] Appointed Lieut. in above Regt. 1 March 1689. Out of the Regt. in 1708.

[24] Ensign's Comn. not forthcoming. Lieut. 23 June 1706. Served at Malplaquet.

[25] Ensign's Comn. not forthcoming. Lieut. 4 May 1707. Served at Malplaquet.

[26] Appointed Ens. in above Regt. 25 Aug. 1704. Served at Malplaquet.

[27] Untraced. Out of the Regt. in 1708.

[28] Ensign's Comn. not forthcoming. Lieut. 24 March 1705. Served at Malplaquet.

[29] Ensign's Comn. not forthcoming. Wounded at Schellenberg. Lieut. 24 March 1705. Adjt. before 1709. Served at Malplaquet.

[30] This officer ought to be among the Captains (see note 11). He was appointed Lieut. in above Regt. 24 March 1691. Adjt. same date. Capt.-Lieut. 30 May 1696. Capt 10 Dec. 1702. Served throughout Marlborough's campaigns and at Sheriffmuir. Promoted Major in 1716. Retired in the following year.

[31] Killed at Schellenberg (*Records*). His Comn. as Ens. is not forthcoming, nor does his Christian name appear in any List.

[32] Appointed Chaplain to above Regt. 1 May 1696. Out of the Regt. 5 Nov. 1711.

[33] See note 21.

[34] Appointed Surgeon to above Regt. 1 May 1696. Present at Malplaquet.

[35] Not in the List of above Regt. for 1709.

LORD NORTH AND GREY'S REGT. OF FOOT.*

COLONEL.

	£	s.	d.	
[Wm.], Lord North and Grey,¹ W. -	144	0	0	Bounty.

LIEUT.-COLONEL.

| [Henry] Groves ² - - - - | 51 | 0 | 0 | ,, |

MAJOR.

| [Jno.] Granville,³ W. - - - | 90 | 0 | 0 | ,, |

CAPTAINS.

[Jno.] Ligonier ⁴ - - - -	30	0	0	,,
[Geo.] Green ⁵ - - - -	30	0	0	,,
[*Alex.*] *Spottiswood*, W. - -	60	0	0	,,
[Sir Jno. Sands,⁶ K.]				
[Geo. Cavendish,⁷ K.]				
[Thos. Burton,⁸ K.] - - -				
[Warner Dawes,⁹ K.] - -				
[Chas. Astley,¹⁰ K.] - -				
[Jno. Cuningham,¹¹ K.] - -				
[Peter Croye,¹² K.] - - -				

CAPT.-LIEUT.

| Wm. Middleton ¹³ - - - - | 14 | 0 | 0 | ,, |

LIEUTENANTS.

[Tho.] Preston ¹⁴ - - -	14	0	0	,,
Giles Stephens ¹⁵ - - -	14	0	0	,,
[Henry] Poilblanc,¹⁶ W. - -	28	0	0	,,
[Saml.] Buller,¹⁷ W. - - -	28	0	0	,,
[Jas.] Sutherland,¹⁸ W. - -	28	0	0	,,
[Granville] Raleigh,¹⁹ W. - -	14	0	0	,,
—— Gay ²⁰ - - - -	14	0	0	,,
[Chas.] Legg ²¹ - - - -	14	0	0	,,
[Jno. Weekes,²² K.] - -				
[Arthur Hornby,²³ K.]				
[Jeremy Freyer,²⁴ K.]				
[Gideon] Ribier ²⁵ - - -	14	0	0	,,

ENSIGNS.

Wm. Lane ²⁶ - - - -	11	0	0	,,
Jno. Rossington ²⁷ - - -	11	0	0	,,
[Constantine] Burton ²⁸ - -	11	0	0	,,
[Wm.] Daniel ²⁹ - - -	11	0	0	,,
[Jno.] Hellows ³⁰ - - -	11	0	0	,,
[Jas.] Scott ³¹ - - - -	11	0	0	,,
[Danl.] Croye,³² W. - - -	22	0	0	,,
[Robt.] Rossington,³³ W. - -	22	0	0	,,
[Walt. Breams,³⁴ K.] - -				
[Thos. Dawson,³⁵ K.]				

CHAPLAIN.

| —— Smith ³⁶ - - - - | 20 | 0 | 0 | ,, |

ADJT.

| Saml. Buller,³⁷ W. - - - | 24 | 0 | 0 | ,, |

THE BLENHEIM ROLL.

	QR.-MR.	£	s.	d.	
[Thos.] Preston [38]	- - - -	14	0	0	Bounty.
	SURGEON.				
[David] Debize [39]	- - - -	12	0	0	,,
	SURGEON'S MATE.				
[Jno.] White [40] -	- - - -	7	10	0	,,

* The 10th Regt. of Foot. The non-commissioned officers and men who received bounty money were 30 sergeants, each of whom received £2; 24 corporals, each of whom received £1 10s.; 476 privates (including drummers) each of whom received £1; 3 sergeants and 36 privates were wounded at Schellenberg, and 13 privates killed in said battle.

[1] Wm. North, 6th Baron North and 2nd Lord Grey. Appointed Capt. and Lt.-Col. in the 1st Foot Guards 14 Feb. 1702. Colonel of the Regt. now known as the 10th Foot 15 Jan. 1703. Had his right hand shot off at Blenheim. Brigdr.-Gen. 1 June 1706. Major-Gen. 1 Jan. 1709. Lt.-Gen. 1 Jan. 1710. Gov. of Portsmouth 5 Sept. 1712. D.s.p. in 1734.

[2] Called "Grove" in the MS. Appointed Capt.-Lieut. to the Royal Fusiliers 1 Aug. 1692. Capt. 20 May 1693. Wounded at the storming of the breach of Terra Nova, Namur, 20 Aug. 1695. Major to Sir Mat. Bridges's Regt. of Foot 2 June 1700. Bt.-Lt.-Col. 6 March 1703. Lt.-Col. of the 10th Foot 25 Apr. 1704. Bt.-Col. 1 Jan. 1706. Wounded at the battle of Oudenarde. Brigdr.-Gen. 12 Feb. 1711. Succeeded Lord North and Grey as Col. of above Regt. 25 June 1715. Attained the rank of Lt.-Gen. 27 Oct. 1735. D. 19 Nov. 1736, aged 71. Bd. in Westminster Abbey.

[3] Appointed Capt.-Lieut. of above Regt. 20 May 1693. Capt. 19 Apr. 1694. Bt.-Major 25 Oct. 1703. Regtal.-Major 25 Apr. 1704. Bt.-Lt.-Col. 1 June 1706. Bt.-Col. 1 Nov. 1711. Served throughout Marlborough's campaigns. Retired in 1715.

[4] 2nd son of Louis Ligonier, Sieur de Monteuquet, a Huguenot. Aftds. the celebrated Sir Jno. Ligonier, K.B., Field-Marshal and Commander-in-Chief, who was created an Irish Viscount 21 Dec. 1757. Advanced to an English Earldom 10 Sept. 1766. Served as a Volunteer in Flanders in 1702. Appointed Capt. in above Regt. 30 March 1703. Bt.-Major 1 July 1706. At Malplaquet he had 22 shots through his clothes. Bt.-Col. 15 Nov. 1711. Served throughout Marlborough's campaigns. Appointed Lt.-Govr. of Fort St. Philip in Minorca 12 Oct. 1713. Lt.-Col. of the 4th Horse (now 3rd D. G.) in 1716. Served as Adjt.-Gen. in the expedition to Vigo in 1719. Colonel of the 8th Horse (now 7th D. G.) 18 July 1720. Brigdr.-Gen. 14 Nov. 1735. Major-Gen. 2 July 1739. Lt.-Gen. 8 Feb. 1743. Was made a Knight Banneret on the field of Dettingen by George II. for conspicuous gallantry. At Fontenoy Ligonier gained fresh laurels. "At Laffeld he preserved the allied army from destruction and enabled it to withdraw in good order by charging the whole line of French cavalry at the head of the British dragoons in which charge his horse was killed, and he himself taken prisoner." General of Horse 30 Dec. 1746. Transferred to the Colonelcy of the 2nd Dragoon Guards 24 July 1749. Col. of the Royal Horse Guards 27 Jan. 1753. Col. of the 1st Foot Guards 30 Nov. 1757. Master-General of the Ordnance 1 July 1759. Field-Marshal Commanding-in-Chief 30 Nov. 1757. D. 28 Apr. 1770, aged 91.

[5] Appointed Ens. in above Regt. 10 Feb. 1693. Lieut. 1 Jan. 1696. Bt.-Capt. 5 Apr. 1704. Capt. 3 Aug. 1704. As senior Capt. performed the duty of Major when serving with above Regt. at the forcing of the French Lines in July 1705 (*War Office MS.*). Major of Col. Pocock's Regt. in 1706. Half-pay in 1713. Major of Sir Chas. Hotham's Regt. of Foot in 1715.

[6] Comn. as Capt. in above Regt. not forthcoming. His widow received £60 bounty money. Under date of 19 Oct. 1695 Luttrell gives the following entry in his *Short Relation of State Affairs*:— "Yesterday morning a duel was fought in Hide Park between Sir Jo. Sandys and Mr. Boteler, both of Ireland, with seconds, the latter was run through the arm in two places, and the seconds ending their dispute came up and prevented further mischief." Vol. III. p. 539.

[7] Comn. as Capt. in above Regt. not forthcoming. He appears to have been unmarried.

[8] A scion of the ancient family of Burton, Derbyshire, of which stock was Robert Burton, author of *The Anatomy of Melancholy*. Appointed Ens. in above Regt. in July 1702. Purchased his Company in above Regt. 25 Apr. 1704 for £300. There are some interesting letters from this officer to Thos. Coke, Esq. M.P., among the MSS. at Melbourne Hall, Derbyshire, which have been printed by the *Historical MSS. Commission*, 12th Report, Appx. Pt. III.

[9] Appointed Ens. in above Regt. 21 Aug. 1691. Lieut. 19 Sept. 1694. Capt. 1 Aug. 1696. Placed on half-pay on the reduction of his Cy. in 1697. Recommissioned Capt. in same Regt. 31 May 1701. £60 bounty money to his child.

[10] Appointed Capt.-Lieut. of above Regt. 13 June 1695. Capt. 12 Feb. 1702. £60 bounty money to his widow.

[11] Appointed Capt.-Lieut. in above Regt. 25 Aug. 1697. Capt's. Comn. not forthcoming. £60 bounty money to his widow.

[12] Appointed Ens. in above Regt. 1 March 1693. Lieut. 1 Jan. 1695. Capt's. Comn. not forthcoming. Killed at Schellenberg.

[13] Appointed Ens. in above Regt. 22 Feb. 1694. Lieut. 4 May 1696. Made Capt. after Blenheim, his Comn. being dated 3 Aug. 1704. Served at Malplaquet. Out of the Regt. in 1715.

[14] Appointed Qr.-Mr. in above Regt. 10 Apr. 1703. Lieut. 3 Aug. 1704. Served throughout Marlborough's campaigns. Comn. renewed by George I.

[15] Appointed Qr.-Mr. to Lord Lovelace's Regt. of Foot 8 March 1689. Lieut. in same Regt. 1 July 1689. Qr.-Mr. to the 2nd Marine Regt. 17 Jan. 1690. 2nd Lieut. in Col. Thos. Brudenell's Regt. of Marines 19 Aug. 1698. Lieut's. Comn. in Lord North and Grey's Regt. of Foot not forthcoming. Capt. in Lord Lovelace's newly-raised Regt. of Foot 12 Apr. 1706. Bt.-Major 5 March 1708. Out of Lord Lovelace's Regt. in 1713. Appointed Capt. in Brigdr.-Gen. Phineas Bowles's Regt. of Dragoons (now 12th Lancers) in 1715.

[16] Appointed Ens. in above Regt. 22 Apr. 1695. Bt.-Capt. 3 Aug. 1704. Capt. 24 Feb. 1705. Served throughout Marlborough's campaigns. Comn. renewed by George I. Serving in 1717.

[17] Appointed Ens. in above Regt. 10 Feb. 1693. Lieut. 11 Apr. 1697. Adjt. in 1702. Capt. 3 Aug. 1704. Resigned the Adjutancy same date. Served throughout Marlborough's campaigns. Bt.-Lt.-Col. 1 Jan. 1712. Comn. renewed by George I. Out of the Regt. in 1717.

[18] Appointed Ens. in above Regt. 28 Feb. 1689. Lieut. 10 Feb. 1693. Out of the Regt. in 1708.

[19] 3rd son of Philip Raleigh, of London, and of Tenchley, Surrey. Appointed Ens. in Sir David Colyear's Regt. of Foot 6 Apr. 1694. Lieut. in Lord North and Grey's Regt. of Foot not forthcoming. Served throughout Marlborough's campaigns. Capt.-Lieut. 26 Sept. 1712. Sold his Comn. in 1717.

[20] Untraced. Possibly " Jonathan Gay," who was appointed Capt. in Col. Owen Wynne's newly raised Regt. of Foot in 1705.

[21] Lieut's. Comn. in above Regt. not forthcoming. Capt. 3 Aug. 1704. Major of Brigade in Flanders 24 Dec. 1710. Bt.-Major 1 Jan. 1712. Served throughout Marlborough's campaigns. Comn. renewed by George I. Appointed Capt.-Lieut., with rank of Lieut.-Col., in the 3rd Regt. of Foot Guards in 1717.

[22] Appointed Lieut. in above Regt. 12 Feb. 1702. £28 bounty money to his widow.

[23] Appointed Ens. in above Regt. 10 Aug. 1696. Lieut's. Comn. not forthcoming. £28 bounty money to his widow.

[24] Appointed Ens. in above Regt. 13 June 1695. Lieut's. Comn. not forthcoming.

[25] Appointed Lieut. in above Regt. 26 Aug. 1697. Out of the Regt. in 1708.

[26] Appointed Ens. in above Regt. 12 Sept. 1695. Out of the Regt. in 1708.

[27] Belonged to the old Derbyshire family of this name. Comn. of Ens. in above Regt. not forthcoming. Out of the Regt. in 1708. Appointed Lieut. in Col. Wm. Watkins's Regt. of Foot, and attained the rank of Capt. before 1713, when he was placed on half-pay.

[28] 2nd son of Fras. Burton of Dronfield, Derbyshire, and cousin to Capt. Thos. Burton of above Regt., who was killed at Blenheim. Bought Tho. Burton's Ensigncy in Apr. 1705. 2nd Lieut. of Grendrs. 25 July 1705. "Cast away in Ostend Bay in 1707." Burke's *Commoners*, Vol. III. p. 271.

[29] Appointed Ens. in above Regt. 1 Apr. 1696. Lieut. 3 Aug. 1704. Served throughout Marlborough's campaigns. Placed on half-pay in 1713.

[30] Appointed Ens. in above Regt. 11 Apr. 1697. Lieut. 3 Aug. 1704. Served at Malplaquet. Out of the Regt. in 1714.

[31] Ensign's Comn. not forthcoming. Lieut. 24 Aug. 1706. Served throughout Marlborough's campaigns. Comn. renewed by George I.

[32] Appointed Ens. in the above Regt. 12 Feb. 1702. 1st Lieut. of the Grendr. Cy. 3 Aug. 1704. Served at Malplaquet. Out of the Regt. in 1714.

[33] Belonged to the old Derbyshire family of this name. Ensign's Comn. not forthcoming. Lieut. 24 Feb. 1705. Served at Ramillies and Oudenarde. Out of the Regt. 1 May 1709.

[34] Probably son of Capt. Walter Breams who left above Regt. in Apr. 1703. Ensign's Comn. not forthcoming.

[35] Ensign's Comn. not forthcoming.

[36] Left the Regt. 23 Feb. 1706.

[37] See note 17.

[38] See note 14.

[39] Appointed Surgeon to above Regt. 10 July 1694. Served throughout Marlborough's campaigns. Comn. renewed by George I. This officer's son, Roger Augustus, was appointed an Ens. in above Regt. 1 Aug. 1711, and in the next reign held an appointment under Lt.-Gen. Wade in Scotland.

[40] Appointed Surgeon to the Rl. Welsh Fusiliers 27 Sept. 1707.

BRIGADIER-GENERAL HOWE'S REGT. OF FOOT.*

LIEUT.-COLONEL COMMANDING.

	£	s.	d.	
Wm. Breton,[1] W. - - - -	144	0	0	Bounty.

MAJOR.
[Fred. Cornwallis,[2] K.]

CAPTAINS.

	£	s.	d.	
Jno. Foulke [3] (or Fowke) - - -	30	0	0	,,
[Chas.] Billingsley [4] - - -	30	0	0	,,
[Thos.] *Whitney* - - -	30	0	0	,,
[Edwd.] Juckes [5] - - -	30	0	0	,,
[Robt. ?] Johnson [6] - - -	30	0	0	,,
[And.] Armstrong,[7] W. - -	60	0	0	,,
[Thos.] Garston,[8] W. - -	60	0	0	,,
[Ric.] Bolton,[9] W. - - -	60	0	0	,,
[Jas. Tancred,[10] K.]				
[Jno. Villeboune,[11] W.]				

CAPT.-LIEUT.

	£	s.	d.	
Wm. Halliday [12] - - - -	14	0	0	,,

LIEUTENANTS.

	£	s.	d.	
[Ric.] Legge [13] - - - -	14	0	0	,,
[Walt.] Sandilands [14] - - -	14	0	0	,,
[Geo.] Sinclair [15] - - -	14	0	0	,,
[Jno.] Calder [16] - - -	14	0	0	,,
[Thos.] Walker [17] - - -	14	0	0	,,
[Jas.] Leslie,[18] W. - -	28	0	0	,,
[Geo.] Morris,[19] W. - -	28	0	0	,,
[Dan.] Dickenson,[20] W. - -	28	0	0	,,
[Henry] Harrison.[21] W. - -	28	0	0	,,
[Robt.] Barton,[22] W. - -	28	0	0	,,
[Wm. King,[23] K.]				
[Wm. Kerr,[24] K.]				
[Thos. Simonds,[25] K.]				

ENSIGNS.

	£	s.	d.	
[Henry] Wingfield [26] - - -	11	0	0	,,
[Edwin] Temple [27] - - -	11	0	0	,,
[Ric.] Lascelles [28] - - -	11	0	0	,,
[Lachlan] Leslie,[29] W. - -	22	0	0	,,
[Edwd.] Hargrave,[30] W. - -	22	0	0	,,
[Ric.] Patrickson,[31] W. - -	22	0	0	,,
[Arthur] Edwards,[32] W. - -	22	0	0	,,
[Thos. Jackson,[33] K.]				
[—— Dean,[34] W.]				
[—— Dawson,[35] W.]				

ADJT.

	£	s.	d.	
Henry Harrison,[36] W. - -	24	0	0	,,

QR.-MR.

	£	s.	d.	
Wm. Halliday [37] - - -	14	0	0	,,

SURGEON.

	£	s.	d.	
[Fras.] de Faure [38] - - -	12	0	0	,,

SURGEON'S MATE.

	£	s.	d.	
[Caleb] Herbert [39] - - -	7	10	0	,,

* The 15th Regt. of Foot. The non-commissioned officers and men who received bounty-money were 38 sergeants, each of whom received £2; 32 corporals, each of whom received £1 10s.; 475 privates (including drummers), each of whom received £1. At Schellenberg this Regt. had 3 officers wounded; 1 sergt. killed and 3 wounded; 9 privates killed and 19 wounded.

[1] Appointed Ens. in the 1st Foot Guards 8 June 1692. Lieut. and Capt. 16 July 1695. Adjt. 1 March 1697. Capt. and Lt.-Col. 3 July 1700. Appointed Lt.-Col. of Col. Emanuel Howe's Regt. of Foot 16 Jan. 1702. Bt.-Col. 2 Aug. 1704. Col. of a newly raised Regt. of Foot 25 March 1705. Brigdr.-Gen. 1 Jan. 1710. Col. of the Regt. now known as the King's Own Borderers 15 Apr. 1711. Appointed Envoy to Prussia in 1711, and took up his residence in Berlin 23 Dec. same year. D. in Dec. 1714 or Jan. 1715.

[2] Appointed Lieut. in Lord Lovelace's Regt. of Foot 8 March 1689. Capt. in the Princess Anne of Denmark's Regt. of Foot (8th Foot) 14 Oct. 1692. Bt.-Major 16 Dec. 1702. Major of Brigdr.-Gen. Howe's Regt. of Foot before 1704. The *Advice to Officers*, printed at Perth in 1795, tells a quaint story of the 15th Foot during the battle of Blenheim:—"One of the senior officers [Major Cornwallis], who knew he was unpopular because of his severity with his men, turned round to them before getting under fire, and confessed he had been to blame, and begged to fall by the hands of the French and not theirs. 'March on, sir,' replied a grenadier, 'the enemy is before us, and we have something else to do than think of you now.' On the French giving way the Major took off his hat and cried, 'Hurrah, gentlemen, the day is our own!' and so saying, he fell dead, pierced through the brain; whether even then accidentally or otherwise by some of his own men, or by the enemy, will never be known."

[3] Appointed Capt. in above Regt. 1 Jan. 1690. Bt.-Lt.-Col. 25 Aug. 1704. This officer petitioned the Duke of Marlborough for preferment in 1706.—"Was present at the battle of Blenheim, since which there has been two Majors and one Lt.-Colonel made to Brigadier Howe's Regt. which he has headed in effect seven years and commanded each of them fifteen. Prays his Grace to do something for him since he has not been a sharer of his Grace's favours upon the battle of Blenheim" (*War Office MS.*). Served throughout Marlborough's campaigns. Serving in March 1712. Out of the Regt. in 1715.

[4] Appointed Lieut. in above Regt. 12 Sept. 1690. Capt. 22 Feb. 1694. Major 25 March 1705. Served in several of Marlborough's campaigns. Out of the Regt. 1 Jan. 1711.

[5] Appointed Ens. in above Regt. 1 March 1690. Lieut. 8 March 1694. Capt. 24 May 1702. Appointed Capt. in Lord Mohun's Regt. of Foot in 1706. Major of Col. Moore's Regt. 7 Apr. 1708. Out of last-named Regt. 28 Apr. 1709.

[6] This officer's Christian name is omitted in the MS. Possibly he was the Capt. Robt. Johnson, or Johnston, whose name appears as Capt. in the Earl of Derby's Regt. of Foot (16th Foot) in the 1702 *Army List*, and of whom nothing further is definitely known.

[7] 3rd son of Edmund Armstrong (*See* Burke's *Baronetage* under "Armstrong of Gallen"). Appointed 2nd Lieut. of an Indep. Cy. of Grenadiers 1 Sept. 1686. Capt.-Lieut. of Col. Sir Jas. Leslie's Regt. of Foot (15th Foot) 1 Nov. 1689. Capt. 1 March 1690. Bt.-Major 1 Oct. 1703. Regtl.-Lt.-Col. 25 March 1705. Bt.-Col. 1 Jan. 1707. Commanded above Regt. at the siege of Tournay and at Malplaquet in 1709. Retired from the Army before 1 Jan. 1715. D. in 1722, aged 80.

[8] Appointed Ens. in above Regt. 1 Apr. 1695. Lieut. 1 Apr. 1697. Capt. 9 March 1699. Served at Malplaquet. Out of the Regt. 1 Jan. 1715.

[9] Appointed 2nd Lieut. of the Grendr. Cy. in Visct. Castleton's Regt. of Foot 1 March 1690. Lieut. 19 Nov. 1691. Adjt. 20 Aug. 1694. Capt.-Lieut. 10 June 1695. Capt. 20 Sept. 1696. Placed on half-pay in 1698. Capt. of a Cy. raised for service and added to Col. Emanuel Howe's Regt. of Foot 12 Feb. 1702. Wounded at Schellenberg. Out of Regt. in 1708.

[10] Appointed Ens. in above Regt. 25 July 1690. Capt. 11 Dec. following. Was senior Capt. of his Regt. at the time of his death. £60 bounty-money to his widow.

[11] This officer's name is omitted in the MS., but he is named in the *Records of the 15th Foot* as having been wounded at Blenheim. The probability is that he died of his wounds before the Bounty Roll was made out. He was appointed Capt. of the Grendr. Cy. in above Regt. 8 March 1694.

[12] Called "Holliday" in the MS. Appointed Ens. in Col. Archd. Douglas's Regt. of Foot (16th Foot) 10 Oct. 1688. Lieut. 21 Feb. 1689. Capt. of the Grendr. Cy. 1 May 1694. Placed on half-pay in 1698. Appointed Lieut. in Col. Emanuel Howe's Regt. of Foot 20 May 1702. Capt.-Lieut. 1 Jan. 1706. Capt. 21 May 1708. Served throughout Marlborough's campaigns. Comn. renewed by George I. Serving in 1717.

[13] Appointed Ens. in the Duke of Bolton's Regt. of Foot 23 March 1697. Lieut. in Sir Hy. Belasyse's Regt. of Foot 6 Sept. 1698. Transferred to Col. Emanuel Howe's Regt. of Foot 10 June 1699. Capt. 1 Feb. 1706. Served throughout Marlborough's campaigns. Comn. renewed by George I.

[14] Appointed Ens. in above Regt. 28 Apr. 1697. Lieut. 2 Apr. 1704. Capt.-Lieut. 24 Oct. 1708. Served at Malplaquet. Out of the Regt. in Jan. 1715.

[15] Appointed Lieut. in above Regt. 12 Apr. 1691. Served at Malplaquet. Out of the Regt. 1 Jan. 1715.

S 8623.

D

¹⁶ Appointed Lieut. in above Regt. 25 Aug. 1704. Killed at the battle of Oudenarde. Left 4 young children entirely dependent on charity. *Treasury Papers*, Vol. CXXX. No. 7.

¹⁷ Appointed Lieut. in above Regt. 25 June 1703. Served at Malplaquet. Out of the Regt. 1 Jan. 1715.

¹⁸ Son of Sir Jas. Leslie (or Lesley) the former Colonel of above Regt. Appointed ensign to the Col.'s Cy. in above Regt. 12 Sept. 1690. Lieut. 18 Jan. 1696. Wounded at Schellenberg. Capt. 25 Aug. 1704. Bt.-Major 1 Jan. 1707. Killed at Malplaquet.

¹⁹ Appointed Ens. in above Regt. 1 March 1690. Lieut. 22 Feb. 1694. Wounded at Schellenberg. Capt. 25 Aug. 1704. Out of the Regt. 21 May 1708.

²⁰ Appointed Ens. in above Regt. 12 Apr. 1691. Lieut. 31 May 1701. Killed in action in Flanders before 1709. See his widow's petition for a pension in *Treasury Papers*, Vol. CXXIV. No. 31.

²¹ Appointed Ens. in above Regt. 22 Feb. 1696. Lieut. and Adjt. before Aug. 1704. Capt. 25 Aug. 1704. Served throughout Marlborough's campaigns. Was made Bt.-Col. for his services 15 Nov. 1711. Regtal.-Lt.-Col. before 1715. Colonel of above Regt. 8 Feb. 1715. Brigdr.-Gen. 9 Nov. 1735. Major-Gen. 2 July 1739. Lt.-Gen. 5 Feb. 1743. D. in 1749.

²² A *protégé* of Lord Halifax (See *Marlborough Dispatches*, Vol. IV., p. 129). Appointed Ens. in above Regt. 18 Jan. 1696. Lieut. 24 May 1702. Adjt. 25 Aug. 1704. Capt.-Lieut. 1 June 1708. Capt. 24 Oct. 1708. Resigned the Adjutancy same date. Served throughout Marlborough's campaigns, and was wounded at the siege of Tournay. Comn. renewed by George I. A certain Capt. Barton "who served under the Duke of Marlborough in all his campaigns" died in 1748 aged 97. *Gent.'s Mag.*

²³ Lieut.'s Comn. in above Regt. not forthcoming. £28 bounty-money to his widow and 4 children.

²⁴ Lieut.'s Comn. in above Regt. not forthcoming. £28 bounty-money to his widow and child.

²⁵ Appointed Lieut. to a Cy. added to Col. Emanuel Howe's Regt. of Foot 31 May 1701. This officer's name is spelt in various ways in the *Comn. Entry Books*.

²⁶ Appointed Ens. to the Colonel's Cy. in above Regt. 1 July 1702. Lieut. and Capt. in the 1st Foot Guards 25 March 1705. Transferred to Brigdr.-Gen. Sterne's Regt. of Foot (Rl. Irish) as Capt. 25 March 1708. Comn. renewed by George I. Attained the rank of Colonel, and d. at Hammersmith in 1736.

²⁷ Appointed Ens. in above Regt. 8 March 1694. Out of the Regt. in 1708.

²⁸ Ensign's Comn. in above Regt. not forthcoming. Lieut. 24 Apr. 1706. Served throughout Marlborough's campaigns. Comn. renewed by George I. Serving in 1717.

²⁹ Appointed Ens. in above Regt. 24 May 1702. According to the "List of all the Brevets granted by the Duke of Marlborough" given at the end of the *MS. Army List*, 1702–1706, this young officer was made Brevet-Captain 25 June 1703. The presumption is that Ens. Leslie temporarily commanded his Cy. in the absence of the Capt. and Lieut. He was promoted Lieut. 25 Aug. 1704. Served at Oudenarde. Out of the Regt. 24 Oct. 1708.

³⁰ Ensign's Comn. in above Regt. not forthcoming. Lieut. 25 Aug. 1704. Served at Malplaquet. Out of the Regt. 1 Jan. 1715.

³¹ Ensign's Comn. in above Regt. not forthcoming. Out of the Regt. 25 March 1708.

³² First Comn. dated 25 March 1704. Ens. to Capt. Harrison's Cy. in above Regt. 25 March 1705. Lieut. 24 Oct. 1708. Served throughout Marlborough's campaigns. Comn. renewed by George I. Capt.-Lieut. in 1715 or early in 1716. Capt. 16 May 1720. Exchanged into the Cavalry and became Major of Horse Grenadiers 21 May 1733. Serving in 1742.

³³ Comn. not forthcoming. £22 bounty-money to his widow and 4 children.

³⁴⁻³⁵ Untraced. These officers are mentioned as having been wounded at Blenheim in the *Records of the 15th Foot*, and probably died before the Bounty Roll was made up.

³⁶ See note 21.

³⁷ See note 12.

³⁸ Appointed Surgeon to above Regt. 19 Dec. 1700. Comn. renewed by George I.

³⁹ Appointed Surgeon to Col. Wm. Breton's Regt. of Foot 24 Aug. 1705. Surgeon to Lord Mohun's Regt. of Foot 15 Apr. 1708.

THE EARL OF DERBY'S REGT. OF FOOT.*

LIEUT.-COLONEL COMMANDING.

	£	s.	d.	
Hans Hamilton,[1] W.	144	0	0	Bounty.

MAJOR.

[Jno. Mordaunt [2] (or Morden), K.]

CAPTAINS.

	£	s.	d.	
Jno. Reddich [3]	30	0	0	,,
Tho. Cooke [4]	30	0	0	,,
Peyton Ventris [5]	30	0	0	,,
Wm. Gooch [6]	30	0	0	,,
Tho. Hesketh,[7] W.	60	0	0	,,
[Michl.] Fleming,[8] W.	60	0	0	,,
[Saml.] Sleigh,[9] W.	60	0	0	,,
[Alex.] Horne,[10] W.	60	0	0	,,
[Garret Coghlan,[11] K.]				

CAPT.-LIEUT.

LIEUTENANTS.

	£	s.	d.	
Tho. Hooke [12]	14	0	0	,,
Pat. Gardiner [13]	14	0	0	,,
[Jno.] Ayloffe,[14] W.	28	0	0	,,
[Ric.] Reddich,[15] W.	28	0	0	,,
[Jno.] Jackson,[16] W.	28	0	0	,,
[Fry] Vicaridge,[17] W.	28	0	0	,,
[Randal Browne,[18] K.]				

ENSIGNS.

	£	s.	d.	
Roderick Bean [19] (or Bayne)	11	0	0	,,
Bryan Stapylton [20]	11	0	0	,,
Robt. Illingworth [21]	11	0	0	,,
Wm. Mackreth,[22] W.	22	0	0	,,
Wm. Hooke,[23] W.	22	0	0	,,
Jno. Kay,[24] W.	22	0	0	,,
[—— Charlton,[25] K.]				
[Jno. Gordon,[26] W.]				
[Wm. Sabine,[27] K.]				
[Jas. Hesketh,[28] K.]				

SURGEON.

[Jno. Whitfield,[29] K.]

SURGEON'S MATE.

	£	s.	d.	
Jas. Dawson [30]	7	10	0	,,

[VOLUNTEER].

[Saml. Harvey [31]]

---

* The 16th Foot. The non-commissioned officers and men who received bounty-money were 34 sergeants, each of whom received £2; 31 corporals, each of whom received £1 10s.; and 567 privates (including drummers), each of whom received £1. The Revd. Wm. Sawle, the veteran Chaplain of above Regt., appears to have been absent during the campaign of 1704.

[1] Appointed Ens. in Col. Archd. Douglas's Regt. of Foot (16th Foot) 15 Oct. 1688. Capt.-Lieut. 31 Dec. 1688. Capt. 21 Feb. 1689. Lt.-Col. 1 Feb. 1697. Bt.-Col. before Aug. 1704. Wounded at Schellenberg. Colonel of the Regt. now known as the 34th Foot 1 Feb. 1706. Served as Qr.-Mr.-General in Spain under Lord Peterborough. Transferred to the Colonelcy of the 16th Foot 23 June 1713. Sold his Comn. 11 July 1715. D. in 1721.

[2] Appointed Qr.-Mr. in above Regt. 1 Aug. 1692. Lieut. 20 May 1693. Capt. 14 Nov. 1694. Major 15 Apr. 1697. Killed at Schellenberg. £90 bounty-money to his widow, who is called "Major Mrs. Morden" in the MS.

[3] Appointed Capt. in Col. Jno. Carne's Regt. of Foot 13 Oct. 1688. Capt. in Col. Hodges's Regt. of Foot (16th Foot) 31 Dec. 1688. Served at Steinkirk and Landen. Bt.-Lt.-Col. 1 Jan. 1706. Served throughout Marlborough's campaigns. Comn. renewed by George I. Left the Regt. in 1717.

[4] Appointed Lieut. in Col. Robt. Hodges's Regt. of Foot 31 Dec. 1688. Capt. 1 Jan. 1692. Served at Steinkirk, Landen, and Namur. Had Marlborough's leave to stay in England during the summer of 1705 on account of ill health; and getting worse, arranged to sell his Comn. for 400 guineas, but died before the business was settled, leaving his family destitute. *War Office MS.*

[5] Appointed Ens. in above Regt. 1 Apr. 1697. Capt. 12 Feb. 1702. Out of the Regt. before 1705.

[6] Eldest son of Thos. Gooch, Alderman of Yarmouth. Appointed Capt. in above Regt. 1 Apr. 1704. Served throughout Marlborough's campaigns. Comn. renewed by George I. Resigned his Comn. in 1717. Appointed Lieut.-Gov. of Virginia in 1727. Colonel of an American Regt. of Foot in 1740. Brigdr.-Gen. same year. Served at the siege of Carthagena and was wounded. Created a Bart. 4 Nov. 1746. D. in 1751.

[7] Appointed Capt. in above Regt. 1 May 1694. Served throughout Marlborough's campaigns. Out of the Regt. in 1715.

[8] 3rd son of Sir Daniel Fleming, Knt., of Rydal Hall, Westmoreland. Appointed Ens. in above Regt. 20 May 1693. Lieut. 12 June 1694. Capt. 25 May 1697. Cy. reduced in 1698. Appointed Lieut. to Lt.-Col. Hans Hamilton in above Regt. 1 July 1699. Capt. 31 May 1701. Bt.-Major 1 May 1708. Served throughout Marlborough's campaigns. Regtal. Major before 1 Jan. 1715. M.P. for Westmoreland. See Burke's *Landed Gentry*, art. "Fleming of Rayrigg."

[9] Appointed Lieut. in above Regt. 20 May 1693. Capt.-Lieut. 25 May 1697. Capt. 6 Sept. 1698. Bt.-Major 1 Jan. 1712. Served throughout Marlborough's campaigns. Comn. renewed by George I.

[10] Appointed Adjt. in above Regt. 12 June 1694. Lieut. 1 July 1695. Served at the siege of Namur. Capt. 20 Feb. 1703. Capt. in Lord Slane's Regt. of Foot in 1708. Placed on half-pay in 1712.

[11] Appointed Capt. in above Regt. 2 Dec. 1695. Wounded at Schellenberg. Killed at Blenheim.

[12] Appointed Ens. in above Regt. 1 May 1694. 2nd Lieut. of the Grendr. Cy. 15 Aug. 1695. Served at the siege of Namur. Capt. 25 Aug. 1704. Served throughout Marlborough's campaigns. Comn. renewed by George I. Serving in 1730.

[13] Of Torwood Head, Linlithgowshire. Appointed Lieut. in above Regt. 31 Dec. 1688. Md. Mary Hodges of Gladsmuir (sister to Col. Robt. Hodges of above Regt., who fell at Steinkirk), and had 2 sons, the younger of whom was the renowned Col. Jas. Gardiner, who fell at Prestonpans, where he commanded the Regt. of Dragoons now known as the 13th Hussars. Col. Jas. Gardiner's biographer says that Lieut. Pat. Gardiner was killed at the battle of Blenheim, but this is evidently a mistake. The probability is that Lieut. Gardiner died soon after the battle.

[14] Appointed Lieut. in above Regt. 31 May 1701. Capt. 29 June 1705. Adjt. before 1708. Wounded at Malplaquet. Out of the Regt. 1 Jan. 1715.

[15] Appointed Lieut. in above Regt. 12 Feb. 1702. Capt.-Lieut. 29 June 1705. Bt.-Capt. 1 May 1708. Capt. 3 Nov. 1708. Served throughout Marlborough's campaigns. Out of the Regt. before 1715. A certain Captain *Reddish* died in London in 1736. *Gent.'s Mag.*

[16] Appointed Lieut. in above Regt. 1 March 1696. Out of the Regt. 1 May 1709.

[17] Appointed Ens. in above Regt. 4 Apr. 1695. Served at the siege of Namur. Lieut. 25 May 1697. Capt. 25 Aug. 1704. Served at Malplaquet. Out of the Regt. in 1715.

[18] Appointed Lieut. in above Regt. 19 Nov. 1692. Served at Landen in 1693.

[19] Appointed Ens. in Col. Æneas Mackay's Regt. of Foot (Scots Brigade) 18 June 1697. Placed on half-pay in March 1698. Ens. in the Earl of Derby's Regt. of Foot about 1702. Lieut. 25 Aug. 1704. 1st Lieut. to Col. Duncan Mackenzie's Indep. Cy. of Foot in Scotland 30 March 1711. Said Cy. was subsequently added to the 3rd Foot Guards. The above officer sold his Comn. as Lieut. and Capt. in 1717.

[20] Belonged to the old Yorkshire family of this name. Appointed Ens. in Col. Jno. Gibson's Regt. of Foot 20 Jan. 1698. Placed on half-pay same year. Ens. in the Earl of Derby's Regt. of Foot 31 May 1701. Out of said Regt. soon after Blenheim.

[21] Obtained his first Comn. as Ens. in the Earl of Drogheda's Regt. of Foot. Ens. in the Earl of Derby's Regt. of Foot 12 Feb. 1702. Lieut. 25 Aug. 1704. Out of the Regt. 24 March 1705.

[22] Appointed Ens. in above Regt. 1 June 1702. Lieut. 29 June 1705. Wounded at Malplaquet. Comn. renewed by George I. Serving in 1730 as Capt.-Lieut. of above Regt.

[23] Appointed Ens. in above Regt. 1 June 1702. Lieut. 25 Aug. 1704. Served throughout Marlborough's campaigns. Capt. 24 Aug. 1715. Major 30 Sept. 1730. Lt.-Col. 15 Dec. 1738. D. in 1762.

[24] "Served seven years in the Horse Guards and three as Lieut. of Grendrs. in above Regt." (*War Office MS.*). Date of Comn. in above Regt. not forthcoming. Lieut. 25 Aug. 1704. "Shot through both thighs and in the right shoulder at Schellenberg." Appointed Capt. of the Grendr. Cy. in Lord Lovelace's Regt. of Foot 12 Apr. 1706. Placed on half-pay in 1713.

[25] Killed at Schellenberg. Christian name and date of his Comn. in above Regt. not forthcoming.

[26] Appointed Ens. in above Regt. 10 July 1697. D. of wounds received at Blenheim. £22 bounty-money to his widow and 3 children.

[27] Appointed Ens. in above Regt. 28 May 1699.

[28] Ensign's Comn. not forthcoming.

[29] Appointed Surgeon in above Regt. 15 March 1697. Surgeon Whitfield was the only medical officer killed at Blenheim. £24 bounty-money to his widow.

[30] Out of the Regt. 3 Nov. 1708.

[31] "Brother to John Harvey of Ickwellbury, in the County of Bedford, Esq. Served the last two campaigns as Volunteer in Colonel Godfrey's Regiment. Prays a Lieutenancy in the New Levys" (Recommendation for a Comn. by Col. Godfrey and others in 1706. *War Office MS.*).

BRIGADIER-GENERAL HAMILTON'S REGT. OF FOOT.*

COLONEL.

	£	s.	d.	
Fred Hamilton	72	0	0	Bounty.

LIEUT.-COLONEL COMMANDING.

Robt. Sterne [1]	51	0	0	,,

MAJOR.

Ric. Kane,[2] W.	90	0	0	,,

CAPTAINS.

Jno. Moyle [3]	30	0	0	,,
Peter D'Offranville [4]	30	0	0	,,
Jos. Stroud [5]	30	0	0	,,
Fred de La Penotière,[6] W.	60	0	0	,,
Moses Leathes,[7] W.	60	0	0	,,
Nat. Hussey,[8] W.	60	0	0	,,
[Henry Browne,[9] K.]				
[Ar. Rolleston,[10] K.]				
[—— Vauclin,[11] W.]				

CAPT.-LIEUT.

Tho. Laughlin [12]	14	0	0	,,

LIEUTENANTS.

Geo. Hall [13]	14	0	0	,,
Jas. Lilly [14]	14	0	0	,,
Robt. Parker [15]	14	0	0	,,
Wm. Leathes [16]	14	0	0	,,
Ben. Smith [17]	14	0	0	,,
Wm. Blakeney [18]	14	0	0	,,
Wm. Weddall,[19] W.	28	0	0	,,
Saml. Roberts,[20] W.	28	0	0	,,
Jno. Harvey,[21] W.	28	0	0	,,

ENSIGNS.

Jno. Blakeney [22]	11	0	0	,,
Henry Walsh [23]	11	0	0	,,
Jno. Cherry [24]	11	0	0	,,
Wm. Rolleston [25]	11	0	0	,,
Saml. Smith [26]	11	0	0	,,
Robt. Tripp [27]	11	0	0	,,
Jas. Pinsent,[28] W.	22	0	0	,,
Stephen Gilman,[29] W.	22	0	0	,,
Edwd. Walsh,[30]	22	0	0	,,
[Wm. Moyle,[31] K.]				

CHAPLAIN.

Henry Reynolds [32]	20	0	0	,,

ADJT.

Wm. Blakeney [33]	12	0	0	,,

QR.-MR.

Edm. Arwaker [34]	14	0	0	,,

SURGEON.

Robt. Weldon [35]	12	0	0	

SURGEON'S MATE.

Robt. Taylor [36]	7	10	0	,,

* The Royal Irish Regt. of Foot. The non-commissioned officers and men who received bounty-money were 32 sergeants, each of whom received £2 ; 36 corporals, each of whom received £1 10s. ; 479 privates (including drummers), each of whom received £1. At Schellenberg the Royal Irish had 1 sergeant killed and 3 wounded ; 11 privates killed and 32 wounded.

¹ Kinsman to Laurence Sterne of Tristram Shandy fame. Appointed Capt. in Sir Jno. Edgeworth's Regt. of Foot (18th Royal Irish) 1 March 1689. Major 22 Dec. 1692. Lt.- Col. 21 Aug. 1695. Served at the sieges of Limerick and Namur. Bt.-Col. 1 Jan. 1706. Brigdr.-Gen. 12 Feb. 1711. Served throughout Marlborough's campaigns, and succeeded to the Colonelcy of above Regt. 18 Feb. 1712. Appointed Gov. of the Rl. Hospital at Kilmainham in 1728. D. in 1732.

² Appointed Lieut. in Col. Skeffington's Londonderry Regt. of Foot 1 Jan. 1689. Lieut. in the Earl of Meath's Regt. (18th Rl. Irish) 12 Nov. 1692. Capt. 25 Sept. 1693. Major 24 Aug. 1704. Wounded at the siege of Namur in 1695. Bt.-Lt.-Col. 1 Jan. 1706. Commanded the Regt. at Malplaquet as Lt.-Col. Appointed Col. of a Regt. of Foot (late Macartney's) 8 Dec. 1710. Lt.-Gov. of Minorca 16 Aug. 1712. Lt.-Gov. of Gibraltar in 1720. Col. of the Regt. now known as the 9th Foot 25 Dec. 1725. Gov. of Minorca in 1730. Brigdr.-Gen. in 1734. D. 20 Dec. 1736 (M. I. in Westminster Abbey). Bd. in St. Philip's Church, Minorca. Author of *Narrative of Campaigns in the Reigns of Wm. III. and Queen Anne*, and *New System of Exercise for a Battalion of Foot* (both published in 1745).

³ Appointed Capt. in above Regt. 4 Jan. 1696. Lt.-Col. of Col. Roger Townshend's Regt. of Foot 12 Apr. 1706. Placed on half-pay in 1713. Lt.-Col. of Col. Wm. Newton's Regt. of Dragoons in 1715. Brigdr.-Gen. 13 Mar. 1727. Major-Gen. 5 Nov. 1735. Col. of the 36th Foot 14 May 1732. Removed to the 22nd Foot 27 June 1737. D. 3 Nov. 1738.

⁴ Appointed Lieut. in above Regt. 7 May 1694. Served at the siege of Namur. Capt. 1 Jan. 1703. Served throughout Marlborough's campaigns. Comn. renewed by George I. Major of above Regt. in 1716. Serving in 1717.

⁵ Appointed Capt. in above Regt. 22 Dec. 1692. Served at the siege of Namur. Out of the Regt. in 1708.

⁶ Appointed Ens. in Prince Geo. of Denmark's Regt. of Foot 14 Sept. 1693. Capt. in Col. Tho. Meredith's Regt. of Foot 13 Feb. 1702. Transferred to the Royal Irish Regt. before Aug. 1704. Bt.-Major 1 July 1706. Regtal.-Major 18 Feb. 1712. Md. Bridget eldest dau. of the Hon. and Rev Jno. Feilding, D.D., youngest son of the Earl of Desmond. Capt. La Penotière, R.N., who fought at Trafalgar, brought home the despatches.

⁷ Probably son of Moses Leathes, appointed Purveyor to the fixed hospital in Ireland 1 Feb. 1690. Capt. of the Grendr. Cy. in Col. Luke Lillingston's Regt. of Foot 22 Dec. 1694. Capt. in the Royal Irish Regt. 24 May 1702. Wounded at Schellenberg. Bt.-Major 1 July 1706. Lt.-Col. of the Royal Irish Regt. 18 Feb. 1712. Bt.-Col. same year. Comn. renewed by George I. Serving in 1717.

⁸ Appointed Ens. in above Regt. 11 Feb. 1696. Ens. in the 1st Foot Guards 12 June 1698. Capt. in the Royal Irish Regt. 1 Apr. 1703. Served at Malplaquet. Out of the Regt. in 1715.

⁹ Appointed Lieut. in above Regt. 24 Sept. 1692. Adjt. 1 Nov. 1693. Capt. 14 Sept. 1695. Served at the siege of Namur. £60 bounty-money to his widow and 3 children.

¹⁰ Appointed 1st Lieut. of the Grendr. Cy. in the Royal Irish Regt. 7 May 1694. Capt.-Lieut. 2 June 1698. Capt. before Aug. 1704. £60 bounty-money to his widow. Called "Arphaxad Rolleston" in the *Flanders Army List* for 1694, but in the List of officers killed at Blenheim his Christian name is given as "Archibald."

¹¹ Christian name and date of Comn. not forthcoming. Died of wounds received at Blenheim. Records.

¹² Appointed Lieut. in the Marquis de Rada's Regt. of Foot 10 Sept. 1694. Lieut. in the Rl. Irish Regt. 1 Apr. 1697. Capt. 24 June 1704. Out of the Regt. 11 Sept. 1708.

¹³ Appointed Ens. in above Regt. 29 Feb. 1696. Lieut. 16 Aug. 1702. Out of the Regt. 28 Aug. 1708.

¹⁴ Called "Little" in the MS. Appointed Ens. in above Regt. 20 May 1695. Served at the siege of Namur. Lieut. 2 June 1698. Capt.-Lieut. 1 Apr. 1707. Capt. 1 May 1708. Served at Malplaquet. Out of the Regt. in 1715.

¹⁵ Son of a Kilkenny farmer. Enlisted in Capt. Fred. Hamilton's Indep. Cy. of Foot in Oct. 1683. This Cy. was added to Lord Mountjoy's Regt. in 1684. Turned out of the Army by Tyrconnell, when the Irish Forces were purged of all Protestant officers and soldiers. Re-enlisted, in London, in March 1689 in Lord Forbes's Regt., which Corps he accompanied to Ireland the same year, and served throughout the Irish campaign. Wounded at the siege of Namur, and given a Comn. in the Royal Regt. of Ireland 16 Dec. 1695. Lieut. in 1702. Adjt. before 1706. Capt.-Lieut. 1 May 1706. Fought at Ramillies. Severely wounded at the siege of Menin. Capt. of the Grendr. Cy. 11 Sept. 1708. Appointed a drill instructor in Ireland (1708), which post he held for 2 years, at the end of which time the Government gave him a gratuity of £200 (Parker's *Memoirs*, p. 148). In Apr. 1718 resigned his Comn. to a nephew of Lt.-Gen. Fred. Hamilton, who paid "a valuable consideration" for the same. See Captain Robert Parker's *Memoirs*, printed in London in 1747.

¹⁶ Appointed Lieut. in above Regt. 10 Feb. 1698. Capt. 1 Jan. 1706. Served throughout Marlborough's campaigns. Comn. renewed by George I. Resigned his Comn. in 1718 to his kinsman, Lieut. Jeremiah Mussenden, of the same Regt.

¹⁷ Appointed Lieut. in above Regt. 9 May 1693. Served at the siege of Namur. Capt. 1 Apr. 1707. Out of the Regt. 1 May 1708.

¹⁸ Eldest son of Wm. Blakeney, of Thomastown, co. Limerick. Appointed Adjt. to above Regt. 9 Feb. 1699. Ens. to an additional Cy. in same corps 31 May 1701. Lieut. 1 Aug. 1701. Capt. 25 Aug. 1704. Bt.-Major 1 Jan. 1707. Lieut. in the 1st Foot Guards 9 March 1708. Capt. and Lt.-Col. in last-named Regt. before 11 Jan. 1715. Col. of the 27th Inniskilling Regt. 27 June 1737. Served as Brigdr.-Gen. in the Carthagena Expedition in 1741. Defended Stirling Castle in 1745. Major-Gen. 30 March 1745. Lieut.-Gen. 11 Sept. 1747. For his gallant defence of Fort St. Philip, Minorca, Blakeney was made a K.B. 27 Sept. 1756, and created Baron Blakeney in the peerage of Ireland a month later. D.s.p. 20 Sept. 1761, aged 91. Bd. in Westminster Abbey.

¹⁹ Appointed Ens. in Visct. Castleton's Regt. of Foot 20 Aug. 1694. Lieut. in the Rl. Irish Regt. 1 June 1698. Capt. 25 Aug. 1704. Served at Malplaquet. Out of the Regt. in 1715.

²⁰ Appointed Ens. in above Regt. 28 Sept. 1693. Lieut. 14 Sept. 1695. Served at the siege of Namur. Out of the Regt. in 1706.

²¹ Appointed Ens. in above Regt. 1 Aug. 1701. Lieut. 16 Oct. 1703. Out of the Regt. 4 July 1708.

²² Younger bro. to Wm. Blakeney of same Regt. (see note 18). Appointed Lieut. in above Regt. 25 Aug. 1704. Served at Malplaquet. Capt. 18 Dec. 1709. Comn. renewed by George I.

²³ First Comn. not forthcoming. Appointed 1st Lieut. of Grendrs. 8 July 1706. Capt. in Col. Thos. Moor's Regt. of Foot 28 Apr. 1709. Placed on half-pay in 1713.

²⁴ First Comn. not forthcoming. Appointed Lieut. 1 Apr. 1707. Served throughout Marlborough's campaigns. Comn. renewed by George I. Serving in 1717.

²⁵ First Comn. not forthcoming. Appointed 2nd Lieut. of Grendrs. 1 Apr. 1707. Served at Malplaquet. Out of the Regt. in 1715.

²⁶ Untraced. Not in any subsequent List.

²⁷ Appointed Ens. in above Regt. 12 Feb. 1702. Lieut. 25 Aug. 1704. Capt.-Lieut. 11 Sept. 1708. Capt. 10 Aug. 1709. Served throughout Marlborough's campaigns. Comn. renewed by George I. Serving in 1718.

²⁸ First Comn. not forthcoming. Wounded at Schellenberg. Lieut. 1 Jan. 1705. Served throughout Marlborough's campaigns. Capt. 20 Feb. 1712. Comn. renewed by George I.

²⁹ Appointed Ens. in above Regt. 1 Aug. 1702. Wounded at Schellenberg. Bt. to act as Lieut. in above Regt. 25 Aug. 1704. Lieut. 1 Jan. 1705. Capt. 23 March 1711. Served throughout Marlborough's campaigns. Comn. renewed by George I. Major of above Regt. 4 Sept. 1734. Serving in 1745.

³⁰ Served previously as Ens. and Qr.-Mr. in Col. Emanuel Howe's Regt. of Foot. Wounded at Schellenberg. Lieut. in above Regt. before 1708. Out of the last-named Regt. 12 Sept. 1708.

³¹ First Comn. not forthcoming.

³² Appointed Chaplain to above Regt. 1 Aug. 1701. Left the Regt. 23 Dec. 1709.

³³ See note 18.

³⁴ Probably son of the former Chaplain of above Regt. Appointed Lieut. in Col. Wm. Breton's Regt. of Foot 25 March 1705. Major of last-named Regt. 10 June 1708. Lieut.-Col. of Major-General Jno. Livesey's Regt. of Foot (12th Foot) 16 Dec. 1710. Out of said Regt. in 1715.

³⁵ Served as Surgeon's Mate to the Regt. of Irish Foot Guards in Ireland prior to 1687, when he, with all other Protestant officers, was turned out of the Army by Tyrconnell. Appointed Surgeon to the Earl of Meath's Regt. (18th Rl. Irish) 1 May 1689. Out of the above Regt. in 1709.

³⁶ Untraced.

BRIGADIER-GENERAL ROW'S REGT. OF FUSILIERS.*

COLONEL.

[Archd. Row, K.] - - - -   £   s.   d.   Bounty.

LIEUT.-COLONEL COMMANDING.

[Jno. Dalyell,[1] K.] - - -

MAJOR.

[Wm. Campbell,[2] K.] - - - -

CAPTAINS.

	£	s.	d.	
[Alex. Straiton,[3] K.] - - -				
Jno. Crauford,[4] W. - - - -	60	0	0	,,
Walter Shairp[5] - - - -	30	0	0	,,
Jas. De Montresor[6] - - -	30	0	0	,,
Henry Erskine[7] - - -	30	0	0	,,
Jas. Campbell[8] - - -	30	0	0	,,
[David Straiton,[9] K.] - - -				
[Jas. Kygo,[10] W.] - - -				

CAPT.-LIEUT.

	£	s.	d.	
Alex. Fairlie,[11] W. - - - -	28	0	0	,,

1ST LIEUTENANTS.

	£	s.	d.	
Florence Kane[12] - - - -	14	0	0	,,
Garret Wall[13] - - - -	14	0	0	,,
[Jno.] Badenoch[14] - - -	14	0	0	,,
Robt. Falconer[15] - - - -	14	0	0	,,
Jno. Dunbar,[16] W. - - -	28	0	0	,,
Jno. Douglas,[17] W. - - -	28	0	0	,,
Jas. Douglas,[18] W. - - -	28	0	0	,,
[Jno. Vandergracht,[19] K.] - -				
[Walter Trevelyan,[20] K.] - -				
[— Hill,[21] K.] - - -				

2ND LIEUTENANTS.

	£	s.	d.	
Robt. Straiton[22] - - - -	11	0	0	,,
[Wm. Campbell,[23] K.] - - -				
Wm. Elliot,[24] W. - - -	22	0	0	,,
Wm. Williams,[25] - - -	11	0	0	,,
Wm. Primrose,[26] W. - - -	22	0	0	,,
Wm. McHenry,[27] W. - - -	22	0	0	,,
Jas. Ogilvie,[28] W. - - -	22	0	0	,,
Henry Gordon,[29] W. - - -	22	0	0	,,
Pat. Maxwell,[30] W. - - -	22	0	0	,,
Jno. Stewart,[31] W. - - -	22	0	0	,,
Saml. Johnston,[32] W. - - -				
Jno. Campbell,[33] W. - - -	22	0	0	,,

ADJT.

	£	s.	d.	
[Chas. Dunbreck[34]] - - -	12	0	0	,,

SURGEON.

	£	s.	d.	
[Alex.] Renton[35] - - - -	12	0	0	,,

SURGEON'S MATE.

	£	s.	d.	
Fras. Brownjohn[36] - - - -	7	10	0	,,

* The Royal Scots Fusiliers. The non-commissioned officers and men who received bounty money were 36 sergeants, each of whom received £2; 38 corporals, each of whom received £1 10s.; and 469 privates (including drummers) each of whom received £1. At Schellenberg the Regt. had 3 officers wounded and a few privates killed and wounded. The loss in the ranks at Blenheim does not appear.

[1] 3rd son of the renowned Genl. Thos. Dalyell, of Binns, C.-in-C. in Scotland. Served some years in the Scots Brigade in Holland, and was transferred 16 March 1688 from a Cy. in Col. John Wauchope's Regt. to a newly-raised Regt. of Foot in Scotland, the command of which was given to the aforesaid Col. Wauchope. Major of Sir David Colyear's Regt. of Foot 1 Sept. 1689. Lt.-Col. of Col. Robt. Mackay's Regt. (21st Scots Fusiliers) 29 May 1695. Bt.-Col. before 1704. Commanded above Regt. at Blenheim, where they led the first attack upon the enemy. £102 bounty money to his widow and 2 children.

[2] Appointed Capt. of the Grendr. Cy. in above Regt. 21 Feb. 1689. Wounded at the battle of Landen. Major 14 Sept. 1693. Bt.-Lt.-Col. before 1704. D. of wounds received at Blenheim. £102 bounty money to his widow.

[3] Appointed Lieut. in above Regt. before 18 Feb. 1684. Capt.-Lieut. 7 March 1692. Served at Steinkirk. Wounded at Landen. Believed to have been father of Capt. David Straiton, of same Regt., who also fell at Blenheim.

[4] Appointed Capt.-Lieut. of above Regt. 1 Feb. 1697. On 11 Jan. 1698 he received the Royal pardon for killing certain persons in 1688 in an encounter in Scotland (*Warrant Book for Scotland*, Vol. XVI.). Capt. 10 Feb. 1703. Adjt. 6 Nov. 1704. Out of the Regt. 24 June 1706.

[5] Of Blance, N.B., who md. the dau. of Sir Thos. Dalyell. Appointed Ens. of above Regt. before 1688. Capt. 1 Jan. 1692. Served at Steinkirk and Landen. Major in 1704. Lt.-Col. 25 Aug. 1706. Left the Regt. 25 Sept. 1708. D. in 1710.

[6] Son of Jacques de Trésor, a Huguenot refugee (Burke's *Landed Gentry*). Appointed Ens. in Col. Jno. Hales's Regt. of Foot 26 Feb. 1691. Transferred to the Scots Foot Guards 1 Sept. 1691. Lieut. and Capt. 22 May 1694. Capt. in the Rl. Scots Fusiliers 25 Feb. 1702. Wounded at Malplaquet. Major of the Royal Scots Fusiliers 1 Oct. 1709. Appointed Lieut.-Gov. of Fort William, in Scotland, where he d. 29 Jan. 1724, aged 56.

[7] Appointed Capt. in above Regt. 25 Feb. 1702. Out of the Regt. in 1706. A certain "Harry Erskine" was appointed Lt.-Col. of Lord Mark Kerr's newly-raised Regt. of Foot in Scotland 29 March 1706.

[8] Appointed Capt. in above Regt. 25 Feb. 1702. Out of the Regt. 25 Oct. 1704.

[9] Appointed Capt.-Lieut. before 7 July 1702. Capt. before Aug. 1704. Believed to have been son of Capt. Alex. Straiton of same Regt. who also fell at Blenheim.

[10] Appointed Capt. in above Regt. 7 March 1692. Wounded at Steinkirk. D. of wounds received at Schellenberg.

[11] Appointed Lieut. in above Regt. 1 Feb. 1697. Capt.-Lieut. 25 Aug. 1703. Capt. 25 Aug. 1704. Killed at Malplaquet.

[12] Appointed Ens. in above Regt. 7 March 1692. Lieut. 1 Aug. 1692. Served at Steinkirk and Landen. Bt.-Capt. 25 Aug. 1704. Capt. 24 Apr. 1706. Left the Regt. 24 Dec. 1707. Capt. of a Cy. of Invalids 3 July 1708. Second Major of Chelsea Hospital 23 Oct. 1712. Capt. of a Cy. of Invalids at Windsor same date. Left the Service in 1715.

[13] Appointed Ens. in above Regt. 1 Aug. 1692. Adjt. before 1693. Wounded at Landen. Lieut. 14 Oct. 1693. Capt.-Lieut. 25 Aug. 1704. Petitioned Marlborough for a Cy. in the New Levies in 1706. Out of the Regt. in 1707.

[14] Appointed Lieut. in above Regt. 1 Aug. 1692. Served at Landen. Qr.-Mr. before 1702. Out of the Regt. in 1706.

[15] Appointed Ens. in above Regt. 1 Aug. 1692. Served at Landen. Lieut. 19 Oct. 1694. Petitioned Marlborough for a Cy. in the New Levies in 1706. Capt. in above Regt. 24 Aug. 1706. Out of the Regt. 1 Jan. 1708. A certain Capt. Falconer d. in Chelsea in 1742.

[16] Appointed Lieut. in above Regt. 1 March 1689. Wounded at Landen. Capt. 25 Aug. 1704. Served throughout Marlborough's campaigns. Out of the Regt. in 1717.

[17] Appointed Ens. in above Regt. 30 May 1694. Lieut. 20 May 1695. Capt. 24 Dec. 1706. Served at Malplaquet. Comn. renewed by George I.

[18] Comn. as 1st Lieut. of Grendrs. in above Regt. not forthcoming. Out of the Regt. in 1708.

[19] Appointed Ens. in above Regt. 7 March 1692. Adjt. 1 Nov. 1692. Served at Steinkirk and Landen. Lieut. before 1695. £28 bounty money to his widow and 2 children.

[20] Appointed Lieut. in Sir Ric. Atkins's Regt. of Foot 29 Jan. 1696. Placed on half-pay in 1698. Appointed 1st Lieut. in the Rl. Scots Fusiliers on the accession of Queen Anne.

[21] Christian name and Comn. not forthcoming.

[22] Appointed Ens. in above Regt. 1 Aug. 1692. Served at Landen. 1st Lieut. 25 Aug. 1704. Served at Malplaquet.

[23] First Comn. not forthcoming. £28 bounty money to his widow.

[24] Appointed Ens. to the Colonel's Cy. in above Regt. 30 May 1694. 1st Lieut. 25 Aug. 1704. Capt. in the Cameronians 10 Nov. 1704. Served at Malplaquet.

[25] Served 5 years in the ranks before obtaining a Comn. Appointed Ens. in above Regt. 2 Apr. 1693. Served at Landen. 1st Lieut. 25 Aug. 1704. Was recommended by Sir Wm. Scawen, his relative, for a Cy. in the New Levies in 1706 (*War Office MS.*). Further services untraced.

[26] Comn. in above Regt. not forthcoming. Out of the Regt. in 1708.

[27] Appointed Ens. in above Regt. 13 Feb. 1697. 1st Lieut. 25 Aug. 1704. Capt.-Lieut. 18 March 1709. Capt. 1 Oct. 1709. Served throughout Marlborough's campaigns. Out of the Regt. in 1717.

[28] Appointed Ens. in above Regt. 20 Feb. 1697. 1st Lieut. of the Grendr. Cy. 25 Aug. 1704. Capt. 1 Oct. 1709. Serving in 1717.

[29] Comn. in above Regt. not forthcoming. Lost a leg at Blenheim. Petitioned Marlborough in 1706 for a Cy. in the New Levies. Out of above Regt. before 1708.

[30] Appointed Ens. in above Regt. 25 Feb. 1702. 1st Lieut. 24 Apr. 1706. Served at Malplaquet.

[31] Appointed Ens. in above Regt. 10 Feb. 1703. 2nd Lieut. of Grendrs. 24 Aug. 1706. Out of the Regt. in 1709.

[32] Comn. in above Regt. not forthcoming. D. of wounds received at Schellenberg.

[33] Comn. in above Regt. not forthcoming. D. of wounds received at Schellenberg. £28 bounty money to his widow.

[34] Appointed Capt.-Lieut. to Col. Mackay's Regt. of Foot 3 Sept. 1695. Adjt. to the Rl. Scots Fusiliers 28 Apr. 1697. Lieut. 18 June 1697. Appears to have resigned his Lieutenancy before Aug. 1704. Retained the Adjutancy until 6 Nov. 1704.

[35] Erroneously called "Robt. Renton" in the MS. Appointed Surgeon to above Regt. in 1702. Surgeon to Lord Mark Kerr's newly-raised Regt. of Foot 29 March 1706.

[36] Untraced.

LIEUT.-GENERAL INGOLDSBY'S REGIMENT OF FUSILIERS.*

COLONEL.

	£	s.	d.	
Ric. Ingoldsby	72	0	0	Bounty.

LIEUT.-COLONEL COMMANDING.

| Jos. Sabine,[1] W. | 102 | 0 | 0 | ,, |

MAJOR.

| [Jas. Ingoldsby,[2] K.] | | | | |

CAPTAINS.

Jas. Jones,[3] W.	60	0	0	,,
Isaac Eyme,[4] W.	60	0	0	,,
Geo. Morgan, W.	60	0	0	,,
Henry Cookman,[5] W.	60	0	0	,,
Ric. Heming[6]	30	0	0	,,
Mat. Pennefather	30	0	0	,,
Newce (?) Jenkins[7]	30	0	0	,,
[—— Harrison,[8] K.]				

CAPT.-LIEUT.

| [—— Ogilvy,[9] K.] | | | | |

1ST LIEUTENANTS.

Ric. Barker[10]	14	0	0	,,
Jno. Paterson,[11] W.	28	0	0	,,
Chas. Richards,[12] W.	28	0	0	,,
Wm. Carrick,[13] W.	28	0	0	,,
Isaac Jevereau, W.	28	0	0	,,
Griffith Jones,[14] W.	28	0	0	,,
Stephen Cadroy,[15] W.	28	0	0	,,
Wm. Aldy,[16] W.	28	0	0	,,
Southwell Pigott,[17] W.	28	0	0	,,
[Constantine Egan,[18] K.]				
[Alex. Fraser,[19] K.]				
[Edwd. Price,[20] K.]				
[Hugh Smith,[21] W.]				

2ND LIEUTENANTS.

Whitfield Sabine[22]	11	0	0	,,
[Reginald Rowlands,[23] K.]				
Jas. Fullerton[24]	11	0	0	,,
Fleetwood Dormer,[25] W.	22	0	0	,,
Edm. Bayly,[26] W.	22	0	0	,,
Ric. Mathews,[27] W.	22	0	0	,,
Ant. Smith[28]	11	0	0	,,

ADJT.

| Jno. Powell,[29] W. | 24 | 0 | 0 | ,, |

CHAPLAIN.

| Wm. Hawtayne[30] | 20 | 0 | 0 | ,, |

QR.-MR.

| Jno. Smith[31] | 14 | 0 | 0 | ,, |

SURGEON.

| Jno. Young[32] | 12 | 0 | 0 | ,, |

SURGEON'S MATE.

| Nich. Peacock[33] | 7 | 10 | 0 | ,, |

* The Royal Welsh Fusiliers. The non-commissioned officers and men who received bounty-money were 29 sergeants, each of whom received £2; 31 corporals, each of whom received £1 10s.; 427 privates (including drummers), each of whom received £1. At Schellenberg this Regt. had 6 sergeants killed and 6 wounded; 60 privates were killed and 165 wounded. There is no return of the loss in the ranks of the Royal Welsh at Blenheim. In the *Daily Courant* for 15 Dec. 1702 is the following:— " Major-General Ingoldsby's Regt. is to be formed into a Regt. of Fusiliers, and will be called the Welsh Regt. of Fusiliers."

1 Grandson of Avery Sabine, Alderman of Canterbury. Appointed Capt.-Lieut. of Sr. Hy. Ingoldsby's Regt. of Foot 8 March 1689. Capt. of the Grendr. Cy. before 18 Oct. 1689. Major of the late Col. Chas. Herbert's Regt. (Rl. Welsh Fusiliers) 13 July 1691. Lt.-Col. 6 June 1695. Bt.-Col. 1 Jan. 1703. Wounded at Schellenberg. Col. of the Rl. Welsh Fusiliers 1 Apr. 1705. Brigdr.-Gen. 1 Jan. 1707. Distinguished himself at the battles of Ramillies and Oudenarde. Major-Gen. 1 Jan. 1710. Lt.-Gen. 4 March 1727. Gen. 2 July 1730. Appointed Gov. of Gibraltar in 1730, and d. there 24 Oct. 1739. Gen. Sabine purchased the estate of Tewin in Herts in 1715, and was interred in Tewin Church in 1739.

2 Comn. as Major not forthcoming. Capt. in above Regt. 18 Aug. 1695. Comn. renewed in 1702. D. of wounds received at Schellenberg.

3 Appointed Capt. in above Regt. 18 December 1689. Served at the siege of Namur. Wounded at Schellenberg. Called Lt.-Col. Jones in the Records. Out of the Regt. in 1706. A certain James Jones was appointed Lt.-Col. of Col. Luke Lillingston's newly-raised Regt. of Foot 25 March 1705, and succeeded to the command of said Regt. 2 June 1708.

4 Appointed Capt. in above Regt. 20 Nov. 1691. Served at Namur. Wounded at Schellenberg. Major 25 Aug. 1704. Served at Malplaquet. Bt.-Lt.-Col. in 1711. Left the Regt. 24 Dec. 1711.

5 Appointed Ens. in Col. Jno. Courthope's Regt. of Foot 23 Apr. 1694. Capt. in Brigdr.-Gen. Tiffin's Regt. of Foot 27 Apr. 1696. Placed on half-pay in 1698. Capt. in the Rl. Welsh Fusiliers 20 Aug. 1701. Bt.-Major 1 Jan. 1706. Left the Army as Major in the last-named Regt. in 1716, " being not able to do duty." *Add. MSS.* 22, 264.

6 Called " Henning " in some Lists. Appointed 1st Lieut. of the Grendr. Cy. in above Regt. 1 June 1695. Served at Namur. Capt. in 1702. Out of the Regt. in 1706. A certain " Richard Hemming " was appointed Capt. *en second* in Lord Mark Kerr's Regt. of Foot about 1708, and was placed on half-pay in 1713.

7 Appointed Lieut. and Capt. in the 1st Foot Guards 13 June 1701. Transferred to the Rl. Welsh Fusiliers before Aug. 1704. Out of the Regt. in 1708. Probably *Newsham* Jenkins.

8 Killed at Schellenberg. His Christian name and date of Comn. do not appear.

9 Appointed Lieut. in above Regt. 27 July 1691. Served at Namur. Capt.-Lieut. before 1704. Killed at Schellenberg. £28 bounty-money to his widow and child.

10 Called " Butler " in the MS. Appointed Ens. in above Regt. 27 July 1691. Lieut. 20 July 1695. Served at Namur. Out of the Regt. in 1708.

11 Appointed Ens. in above Regt. 1 July 1693. Lieut. 25 July 1695. Wounded at the siege of Namur. Capt. 18 Oct. 1704. Served at Malplaquet. Major in 1710. Promoted Lt.-Col. of above Regt. 24 Dec. 1711.

12 Appointed Ens. in above Regt. 1 Apr. 1696. 1st Lieut.'s Comn. not forthcoming. Wounded at Schellenberg. Out of the Regt. in 1709.

13 Appointed Ens. in above Regt. 22 May 1694. Served at Namur. 1st Lieut. before 1704. Wounded at Schellenberg. Out of the Regt. 24 Sept. 1708.

14 Appointed 1st Lieut. of the Grendr. Cy. in above Regt. 25 Aug. 1704. Served throughout Marlborough's campaigns. Capt. in Oct. 1709. Serving in above Regt. in 1718.

15 Appointed Ens. in above Regt. 19 Apr. 1696. 1st Lieut. 25 Apr. 1703. Wounded at Schellenberg. Capt.-Lieut. 24 Nov. 1708. Served at Malplaquet.

16 Appointed Ens. in above Regt. 1 Nov. 1701. 1st Lieut.'s Comn. not forthcoming. Wounded at Schellenberg. Capt. in Col. Luke Lillingston's newly-raised Regt. of Foot 25 March 1705. Major in 1707. Out of last-named Regt. in 1710.

17 Of Capard, Queen's County. Wounded at Schellenberg. Promoted Capt. in above Regt. 24 Dec. 1705. Served at Malplaquet. Md. Henrietta Wynanda Vandergraff, and had issue. Will dated 18 May 1751, and proved 24 Sept. 1756. See Burke's *Landed Gentry.*

18 Appointed Ens. in above Regt. 22 May 1694. Served at Namur. Lieut. 23 July 1695. Killed at Schellenberg. £28 bounty-money to his widow.

19 Appointed Lieut. in above Regt. 1 Feb. 1694. Served at Namur. Killed at Schellenberg. £28 bounty-money to his widow and 5 children.

20 Appointed Ens. in above Regt. 20 May 1693. Qr.-Mr. 1 Nov. 1694. Served at Namur. Lieut. 23 July 1695. Killed at Schellenberg.

21 Appointed 2nd Lieut. to the Grendr. Cy. in Col. Ric. Coote's Regt. of Foot 1 Nov. 1694. Lieut. to an additional Cy. in the Rl. Welsh Fusiliers 31 May 1701. D. of wounds received at Blenheim.

22 Appointed 2nd Lieut. in above Regt. 24 Aug. 1702. Out of the Regt. in 1708. He was son of the above Col. Jos. Sabine by his first wife.

[23] £24 bounty-money to his widow. In *Treasury Papers*, Vol. CLI., No. 38, under date of 5 Sept. 1712, is a memorial from Elizabeth Rowlands, widow of above officer, praying for a pension, her husband having been killed at Blenheim. The Secretary at War reported to the Lord High Treasurer that " the pension fund was exhausted, but the Queen had directed that a man per troop should be mustered under a fictitious name, whereby the fund for the Flanders widows would be enlarged, and the pensions paid more regularly."

[24] First Comn. not forthcoming. 2nd Lieut. of the Grendr. Cy. in above Regt. 24 June 1706. Killed at Malplaquet.

[25] First Comn. not forthcoming. Was dangerously wounded at Blenheim, and in 1706 was recommended for a Cy. in the New Levies. Appointed Capt. of the Grendr. Cy. in Sr. Roger Bradshaigh's Regt. of Foot 12 Apr. 1706. Left last-named Regt. as Major 30 Dec. 1711.

[26] First Comn. not forthcoming. Capt.-Lieut. of above Regt. 24 June 1706. Out of the Regt. 24 Nov. 1708.

[27] Comn. as 2nd Lieut. in above Regt. dated 25 Aug. 1704. Left the Regt. 23 Feb. 1709.

[28] Comn. not forthcoming. Applied for a Cy. in the New Levies in 1706 (*War Office MS.*). Out of the Regt. in 1708. A certain Anthony Smith was appointed Lieut. in Lord Mark Kerr's Regt. of Foot 23 Nov. 1709.

[29] Appointed Adjt. to above Regt. 25 Aug. 1704. 1st Lieut. 25 Apr. 1706. Wounded at Malplaquet. Capt. 24 Dec. 1711. Cy. reduced in 1713. On half-pay in 1714.

[30] Son of the Revd. Wm. Hawtayne, of Farthingho, Northants. Appointed Chaplain to above Regt. 1 June 1703. Serving in Flanders in 1709. Appointed Rector of Datchworth in 1709, and was subsequently Chaplain to Princess Caroline of Wales until she became Queen.

[31] Out of the Regt. in 1708.

[32] Appointed Surgeon to above Regt. 14 May 1699. Out of the Regt. 24 Sept. 1707. Surgeon to the Rl. Irish Regt. of Foot in 1708.

[33] Untraced.

THE DUKE OF MARLBOROUGH'S [LATE] REGT. OF FOOT.*

LIEUT.-COLONEL COMMANDING.

	£	s.	d.	
Wm. Tatton [1]	72	0	0	Bounty.

MAJOR.

| [Pat.] Meade [2] | 51 | 0 | 0 | ,, |

CAPTAINS.

[Thos.] Oldfield [3]	30	0	0	,,
[Geo.] *Watkins*	30	0	0	,,
[Tho.] Pollexfen,[4] W.	60	0	0	,,
[Jno.] Lacoude,[5] W.	60	0	0	,,
[Vere Fitzsimmons,[6] K.]				
[Tho. Gardiner,[7] W.]				
[Jno. Bayly,[8] W.]				
[Ben. Tichborne,[9] K.]				

CAPT.-LIEUT.

LIEUTENANTS.

[Jno.] Ray [10]	14	0	0	,,
[Fras.] Mallery [11]	14	0	0	,,
[Dan.] Bright [12]	14	0	0	,,
[Jno.] Whitehall [13]	14	0	0	,,
[Jno.] Finch,[14] W.	28	0	0	,,
Jno. Parrot,[15] K.	28	0	0	,,
[Thos.] Albritton,[16] W.	28	0	0	,,
[Jno.] Walley,[17] W.	28	0	0	,,
[Abr.] Stapleton,[18] W.	28	0	0	,,
[Jno.] Ramsay [19]	14	0	0	,,

ENSIGNS.

[Wm. ?] Lancaster [20]	11	0	0	,,
[Wm.] Warren [21]	11	0	0	,,
[Jno.] Parr [22]	11	0	0	,,
[Tim.] Thomas [23]	11	0	0	,,
[Ralph] Ramsay [24]	22	0	0	,,
[Jno.] Douglas,[25] W.	11	0	0	,,
[Hen.] Berkeley [26]	11	0	0	,,
[Jno.] Ballard [27]	11	0	0	,,
[Jno.] Burton [28]	11	0	0	,,
[Saml.] Furnesse,[29] W.	22	0	0	,,
[Jno.] Gardiner [30]	11	0	0	,,

CHAPLAIN.

| [Peter] Maturin [31] | 20 | 0 | 0 | ,, |

ADJT.

| —— Davis [32] | 12 | 0 | 0 | ,, |

QR.-MR.

| [Peter] Groffey [33] | 14 | 0 | 0 | ,, |

SURGEON.

| [Peter] Carnac [34] | 12 | 0 | 0 | ,, |

SURGEON'S MATE.

| [Jas.] Dobbins [35] | 7 | 10 | 0 | ,, |

* The 24th Regt. of Foot. The non-commissioned officers and men who received bounty-money were 32 sergeants, each of whom received £2; 15 corporals, each of whom received £1 10s.; and 442 privates (including drummers), each of whom received £1.

[1] Appointed Ens. in Col. Hy. Cornewall's Regt. (9th Foot) 19 June 1685. Lieut. 1 June 1687. Capt. in 1689. Bt.-Lt.-Col. 7 March 1692. Served in Ireland and Flanders under Wm. III. Lt.-Col. of Col. Sam. Venner's Regt. (24th Foot) 7 Aug. 1695. Bt.-Col. 1 March 1703. Col. of last-named Regt. 25 Aug. 1704. Sold his Colonelcy in 1708. Brigdr.-Gen. 1 Jan. 1707. Major of 1st Foot Guards 9 March 1708. Major-Gen. 1 Jan. 1710. Lt.-Col. of the 1st Foot Guards 12 Oct. 1722. Lt.-Gen. 3 March 1727. Col. of the Buffs 24 Nov. 1729. D. in 1737, at which time he held the post of Gov. of Tilbury Fort.

[2] 3rd son of Lt.-Col. Wm. Meade, of Ballintubby, co. Cork. Appointed Capt. in above Regt. at its first raising on 8 March 1689. Served in Ireland and on board the Fleet. Major 18 Oct. 1695. Lt.-Col. of above Regt. 25 Aug. 1704. Bt.-Col. 1 Jan. 1706. Served at Ramillies. Fought at Malplaquet. Brigdr.-Gen. 12 Feb. 1711. D. in 1732. Will dated 9 Apr. 1726. Proved 30 June 1732.

[3] Served in 1686 as Capt.-Lieut. in Col. Theodore Russell's Regt. of Foot in Ireland. Served in Ireland and on board the Fleet. Bt.-Major 1 Oct. 1703. Major 25 Aug. 1704. Bt.-Lt.-Col. 1 Jan. 1706. Bt.-Col. 1 Nov. 1711. Served throughout Marlborough's campaigns.

[4] Appointed Capt. in above Regt. 20 March 1694. Bt.-Major 1 Jan. 1706. Bt.-Lt.-Col. 1 Jan. 1712. Served throughout Marlborough's campaigns. Regtal.-Major before 1715. Serving in Ireland with the Brevet rank of Colonel in 1724.

[5] Appointed Capt. in above Regt. 19 Feb. 1697. Cy. reduced in 1698. Re-appointed Capt. 28 May 1701. Served at Malplaquet.

[6] Appointed Lieut. in above Regt. 16 Feb. 1694. Capt.-Lieut. 1 March 1697. Capt. in 1702. £60 bounty-money to widow.

[7] Appointed Capt. in above Regt. 18 Feb. 1697. Cy. reduced in 1698. Re-appointed Capt. 28 May 1701. D. of wounds received at Blenheim. £60 bounty-money to his widow.

[8] Appointed Capt. in above Regt. 25 Nov. 1697, having exchanged with Capt. Edm. Harris from Col. Geo. Hamilton's Regt. of Foot. D. of wounds received in the campaign of 1704.

[9] 2nd son of Sr. Wm. Tichborne, of Beaulieu, co. Louth. Appointed Lieut. and Adjt. in above Regt. 8 March 1689. Capt. before Aug. 1692. Served with his Regt. on board the Fleet in 1693. £60 bounty-money to his widow, who was dau. of Major Edwd. Gibbs, of Gloucester, by whom he left 3 children.

[10] Appointed Ens. in Lord Lovelace's Regt. of Foot 8 March 1689. Qr.-Mr. to the Marquis de Puisar's Regt. (24th Foot) 1 Jan. 1699. Lieut. 25 Apr. 1703. Served at Ramillies. Out of the Regt. 24 Oct. 1706.

[11] Appointed Lieut. in above Regt. 18 Aug. 1695. "A French gentleman who had suffered much for his religion." Was recommended for a Cy. in the New Levies in 1706 (*War Office MS.*). Serving in above Regt. in 1709. Believed to have been present at Malplaquet.

[12] Appointed Lieut. in above Regt. 8 March 1689. Out of the Regt. in 1708.

[13] Appointed Ens. in the Coldstream Guards 17 July 1694. 2nd Lieut. in Col. Wm. Seymour's Regt. of Marines 19 Aug. 1698. Transferred as Lieut. to Col. Wm. Seymour's Regt. of Foot 31 May 1701. 2nd Lieut. of Grendrs. in Col. Nich. Price's Regt. of Foot in 1706. Placed on half-pay in 1713.

[14] Appointed Ens. in Lord Cutts's Regt. of Foot 1 Apr. 1692. Lieut. 28 June 1693. Served several campaigns in Flanders under Wm. III. Lieut. in the Earl of Marlborough's Regt. of Foot 12 Feb. 1702. Out of the Regt. in 1708.

[15] Appointed Adjt. in above Regt. 1 May 1694. Lieut. 1 March 1697. £28 bounty-money to his 3 children.

[16] Appointed Ens. in above Regt. 23 Apr. 1694. Lieut. before 1704. Capt. 18 June 1705. Served throughout Marlborough's campaigns. Comn. renewed by George I. as Capt. of the Grendr. Cy. in above Regt. Serving in Ireland in 1724.

[17] Appointed Lieut. in above Regt. 18 Aug. 1695. Out of the Regt. in 1708.

[18] Appointed 1st Lieut. of the Grendr. Cy. in above Regt. before 1709. Served at Malplaquet.

[19] Appointed Ens. to Lt.-Col. Ramsay's Cy. in above Regt. 16 Feb. 1694. Lieut. before Aug. 1704. Out of the Regt. in 1708. A certain Jno. Ramsay was appointed Capt.-Lieut. of Col. De Magny's Regt. of Foot in Portugal in 1709.

[20] Comn. not forthcoming. A certain Wm. Lancaster was appointed Ens. in the 1st Foot Guards 23 Dec. 1706.

[21] Comn. not forthcoming. Out of the Regt. in 1708.

[22] Comn. not forthcoming. Lieut. 25 March 1705. Served throughout Marlborough's campaigns. Comn. renewed in 1715. Capt. before Nov. 1724.

[23] Appointed Ens. in above Regt. 18 Aug. 1695. Lieut. 25 Aug. 1704. Served throughout Marlborough's campaigns. Comn. renewed by George I.

²⁴ Appointed Ens. in above Regt. 1 May 1694. 2nd Lieut. of the Grendr. Cy. 24 Aug. 1704. Served throughout Marlborough's campaigns.

²⁵ Appointed Ens. in above Regt. 7 Aug. 1695. Lieut. 25 Aug. 1704. Served throughout Marlborough's campaigns. Capt.-Lieut. before Jan. 1715.

²⁶ Appointed Ens. in the above Regt. 1 June 1702. Adjt. 24 Feb. 1708. Lieut. 24 Oct. 1708. Served throughout Marlborough's campaigns. Comn. renewed by George I. Capt. and Lt.-Col. in the 3rd Foot Guards 22 July 1715. Attained the rank of Brigdr.-General, and d. at Bath in 1736.

²⁷ Appointed Ens. in above Regt. 1 June 1703. Served at Malplaquet. Out of the Regt. in 1715.

²⁸ Ensign's Comn. not forthcoming. Lieut. 25 Aug. 1704. Capt.-Lieut. 24 Apr. 1708. Served throughout Marlborough's campaigns. Placed on half-pay as Capt. in 1713. Restored to full pay in 1715, but his Cy. reduced 23 Nov. 1717. Living in 1722.

²⁹ Kinsman to Sr. Hy. Furnesse, Bt., of Waldershare, Kent. Appointed Ens. in above Regt. 27 Feb. 1703. Served at Malplaquet. Out of the Regt. in 1715.

³⁰ Ensign's Comn. not forthcoming. Served at Malplaquet. Lieut. before 1715.

³¹ Comn. not forthcoming. Served throughout Marlborough's campaigns. Comn. renewed by George I.

³² Comn. not forthcoming. Out of the Regt. 24 March 1705.

³³ Appointed Qr.-Mr. to the 1st Batt. Rl. Regt. of Foot 14 Apr. 1702 (his original Comn. was lately in the possession of J. Coleman, bookseller, Tottenham). Qr.-Mr. to the Duke of Marlborough's Regt. of Foot 1 May 1704. Lieut. in last-named Regt. 25 Oct. 1704. Bt.-Capt. 1 July 1706. Out of the Regt. in 1715. His son, Jno. Groffey, was given an Ensign's Comn. by Marlborough in 1706.

³⁴ Appointed Surgeon to above Regt. 25 July 1699. Served throughout Marlborough's campaigns.

³⁵ Appointed Surgeon to Col. Heyman Rooke's Regt. of Foot in 1706.

BRIGADIER-GENERAL FERGUSON'S REGT. OF FOOT.*

COLONEL.

	£	s.	d.	
[Jas.] *Ferguson*	72	0	0	Bounty.

LIEUT.-COLONEL COMMANDING.

| [Alex.] Livingston,[1] W. | 102 | 0 | 0 | ,, |

MAJOR.

| [Wm.] Borthwick [2] | 45 | 0 | 0 | ,, |

CAPTAINS.

[Jas.] Cranston [3]	30	0	0	,,
[And.] Monroe [4]	30	0	0	,,
[Jas.] Aikman [5]	30	0	0	,,
[Wm.] Drummond [6]	30	0	0	,,
[Jno.] Blackader,[7] W.	60	0	0	,,
[Henry] Borthwick,[8] W.	60	0	0	,,
[Jas.] Lawson,[9] W.	60	0	0	,,
[Alex. Campbell,[10] K.]				
[Henry Stewart.[11] K.]				

CAPT.-LIEUT.

| [Jno.] Wilson,[12] W. | 14 | 0 | 0 | ,, |

LIEUTENANTS.

[Pat.] Dickson [13]	14	0	0	,,
[Archd.] Wilson [14]	14	0	0	,,
[Geo.] Douglas [15]	14	0	0	,,
[Fras.] Lindsay [16]	14	0	0	,,
Jno. Ferguson [17]	14	0	0	,,
[Tho.] Drummond [18]	14	0	0	,,
—— Wemyss [19]	14	0	0	,,
Mat. Bernard [20]	14	0	0	,,
Robt. Ferguson,[21] W.	28	0	0	,,
Leond. Ferguson,[22] W.	28	0	0	,,
[Geo. Seton,[23] K.]				
[Henry Moncreif,[24] K.]				
[Archd. Douglas,[25] K.]				

ENSIGNS.

[Jas.] Simpson [26]	11	0	0	,,
[Jno.] Dalrymple,[27] W.	22	0	0	,,
[Pat.] Oliphant,[28] W.	22	0	0	,,
—— Marshall,[29] W.	22	0	0	,,
[Alex.] Ogilvie,[30] W.	22	0	0	,,
[Pat. Bernard,[31] K.]				
[Jas. Hay,[32] K.]				
[Chas. Maclean,[33] K.]				
[—— Balfour,[34] K.]				
[—— Low,[35] K.]				

CHAPLAIN.

| [David] Pitcairn [36] | 20 | 0 | 0 | ,, |

ADJT.

| —— Forrest [37] | 12 | 0 | 0 | ,, |

		£	s.	d.	
QR.-MR.					
[Robt.] Stevenson,³⁸ W.	- - -	28	0	0	Bounty.
SURGEON.					
——— Stewart ³⁹	- - - -	12	0	0	„
SURGEON'S MATE.					
——— Man (sic) ⁴⁰	- - - -	7	10	0	„

* The Cameronians. The non-commissioned officers and men who received bounty-money were 33 sergeants, each of whom received £2; 31 corporals, each of whom received £1 10s.; 546 privates (including 24 drummers), each of whom received £1. Only a detachment of this Regt. (numbering 130 men) served at Schellenberg. One sergt. and 18 privates were killed at Schellenberg; 3 sergts. and 57 privates wounded. At Blenheim 1 sergt. and 2 corporals were wounded; 16 privates killed.

¹ Younger bro. to Visct. Teviot, at whose death in 1711 he succeeded to the baronetcy only. Prior to the Revolution served as Capt. in Col. Balfour's Regt. in the Scots Brigade and accompanied the Prince of Orange to England. Served in Scotland. Taken prisoner at Landen. Appointed Lt.-Colonel of the Cameronians 1 Sept. 1693. Bt.-Col. 25 Aug. 1704. Sold the Lt.-Colonelcy of above Regt., but retained his own Cy., 24 Oct. 1705. Placed on half-pay as Capt. in 1713. Md. Mary, dau. of Wm. Borthwick of Pilmuir, and d.s.p.

² Of Johnstonburn. Son of Major Wm. Borthwick. Wounded at the defence of Dunkeld in 1689. Appointed Capt. of the Grendr. Cy. in the Cameronians in Apr. 1689. Major 1 Aug. 1692. Served at Steinkirk and Landen. Served at Schellenberg, but absent on order at Blenheim. Col. of above Regt. 24 Oct. 1705. Exchanged with Lord Dalrymple (Earl of Stair) to the Colonelcy of a Dutch Regt. 1 Jan. 1706. Killed at Ramillies.

³ Son and heir of Jno. Cranston of Glen. Appointed Lieut. in above Regt. in Apr. 1689. Capt.-Lieut. before Aug. same year. Capt. 1 Aug. 1692. Served several campaigns under Wm. III. Commanded the Grendr. Cy. at Blenheim. Lt.-Col. of above Regt. 24 Oct. 1705. Bt.-Col. 1 Jan. 1707. Killed at Malplaquet.

⁴ Probably son of Col. And. Monroe, a former Colonel of this Regt. Appointed Capt.-Lieut. 1 Aug. 1692. Capt. 10 Sept. 1693. Out of the Regt. in 1709.

⁵ Appointed Lieut. in above Regt. in Apr. 1689. Capt. 7 May 1694. Served at Schellenberg. Absent on order at Blenheim. Served at Ramillies and Malplaquet.

⁶ Served in Major Geo. Wishart's Tp. in Lord Jedburgh's Regt. of Dragoons prior to 15 Mar. 1693, when he was qualified to act as Captain in same Regt. by special Wt. from Wm. III., "for the good service done to their Majesties." Capt. of Major Wishart's Tp. 18 Dec. 1693. Capt. in the Cameronians 7 July 1702. Bt.-Major 1 Jan. 1712.

⁷ 5th son of the Revd. Jno. Blackader, Minister of Troqueer. Bn. at Glencairn, Dumfries-shire, 14 Sept. 1664. Appointed Lieut. in above Regt. in Apr. 1689. Capt. 14 Jan. 1693. Served in all the engagements and battles in which his Regt. took part in Flanders. Major 24 Oct. 1705. Lt.-Col. 28 Oct. 1709. Served throughout Marlborough's campaigns. Sold his Comn. after the siege of Bouchain. Commanded a Regt. of Glasgow Volunteers in the Rebellion of 1715. Dep.-Gov. of Stirling Castle 25 Feb. 1717. D. 31 Aug. 1729. Bd. in the West Church, Stirling. Left a valuable MS., which was printed many years after his death, and is known as the *Life and Diary of Lt.-Colonel J. Blackader*.

⁸ Son of Wm. Borthwick of Pilmuir by his 2nd wife. Appointed Capt. in above Regt. 5 May 1702. Killed at Ramillies. By his wife Mary, dau. of Sir Robt. Pringle, of Stichill, Bt., this officer left 2 sons, the younger of whom, Henry, became 11th Baron Borthwick in 1727. Burke's *Peerage*.

⁹ Appointed Ens. in above Regt. 1 Apr. 1691. Lieut. 7 May 1694. Capt. 1 June 1704. Slightly wounded at Schellenberg, also at Blenheim. Served throughout Marlborough's campaigns. Regtal.-Major in 1711. Bt.-Lt.-Col. 1 Jan. 1712. Wounded at the battle of Preston in 1715. Sold his Majority 12 June 1717, to Capt. Robt. Ferguson of the same Regt.

¹⁰ Appointed Capt. in above Regt. 1 Aug. 1693. This officer must not be confounded with Capt. Alex. Campbell of Finab whose Indep. Cy. of Foot "for the security of the Highlands" was temporarily added to the Cameronian Regt. 24 June 1701.

¹¹ Appointed Lieut. in above Regt. in Apr. 1689. Capt. 1 Apr. 1691. Wounded at the battle of Landen. This officer's name is given as "Stuart" in some Lists.

¹² Appointed Ens. in above Regt. in Apr. 1689. Lieut. 1 Aug. 1692. Was 1st Lt. of the Grendr. Cy. in 1702. Capt.-Lt.'s Comn. not forthcoming. Capt. 25 Aug. 1704. Served throughout Marlborough's campaigns.

¹³ Appointed Ens. in above Regt. 1 Apr. 1691. Lieut. 16 June 1697. Capt. 1 Aug. 1706 Served throughout Marlborough's campaigns.

¹⁴ Appointed Ens. in above Regt. in Apr. 1689. Lieut. 2 Apr. 1693. Out of the Regt. in 1708.

¹⁵ Appointed Ens. in above Regt. 7 May 1694. Lieut. 9 May 1703. Bt.-Capt. 1 Dec. 1708. Held the post of Adjt. prior to Dec. 1708. Served throughout Marlborough's campaigns.

¹⁶ Appointed Ens. in above Regt. 1 Aug. 1693. Lieut. 30 May 1696. Out of the Regt. in 1708.

¹⁷ Appointed Ens. in above Regt. 16 June 1697. Adjt. in 1700. Lieut. in 1702. Out of the Regt. in 1708.

¹⁸ Probably kinsman to Brigadier Ferguson's first wife. Appointed Ens. to the Colonel's Cy. in above Regt. 8 May 1696. Lieut. with Brevet of Capt. 1 Sept. 1707. Served throughout Marlborough's campaigns.

¹⁹ Comn. not forthcoming. Out of the Regt. in 1708.

²⁰ Comn. not forthcoming. Served at Ramillies. Capt. 1 Aug. 1706. Present at Malplaquet.

²¹ Nephew to Brigadier Ferguson. Appointed Lieut. in above Regt. 1 June 1693. Served at Landen. Dangerously wounded at Blenheim and not expected to recover (*Memorial*). Capt. 1 Aug. 1706. Served at Ramillies, Oudenarde, and Malplaquet. Fought at Preston in 1715. Purchased the Majority from Lt.-Col. Lawson 12 June 1717, and later bought the Lt.-Colonelcy from Lt.-Col. Jno. Hope 5 Apl. 1718. The high prices paid for these Comns. involved Lt.-Col. Ferguson in very serious money difficulties. About 1730 he memorialised the Principal Secretary of State to the effect that he might be allowed to dispose of his Lt.-Colonelcy so as to pay his debts, and that his Majesty would be pleased to confer on him "some small Government either in Britain or Ireland" so that he might provide for his young family and sickly wife (Undated *Memorial*, Public Record Office). D. 15 Dec. 1738.

²² Appointed Ens. in above Regt. 7 May 1694. Lieut. 24 Aug. 1697. Out of the Regt. in 1708.

²³ Called "Seaton" in the MS. Appointed Ens. in above Regt. 16 June 1697. Lieut. before 1704. D. of wounds received at Schellenberg. £28 bounty money to his widow and 3 children.

²⁴ Appointed Ens. to Col. Ferguson's own Cy. in above Regt. 5 May 1702, "with a clause of precedency from 1 Jan. 1702" (*Warrant Book for Scotland*, Vol. XVIII.). £28 bounty money to widow and 1 child.

²⁵ Lieut. in above Regt. before July 1702.

²⁶ Ensign's Comn. not forthcoming. Lieut. 1 June 1704 (antedated). Served at Malplaquet.

²⁷ 2nd son of the Hon. Wm. Dalrymple, who was brother to the 2nd Earl of Stair. Ensign's Comn. not forthcoming. Lieut. 25 Aug. 1704. Wounded at the attack on the French lines in 1705. Served throughout Marlborough's campaigns. Capt.-Lieut. 19 June 1710. Capt. 27 Oct. 1712. Placed on half-pay in 1713. Appointed Capt. in the Inniskilling Dragoons before 1722. D. in 1742.

²⁸ Possibly the Hon. Pat. Oliphant, who succeeded as 8th Baron Oliphant and d. in 1721. Appointed Ens. in above Regt. 1 June 1704. Served at Ramillies and Oudenarde. Out of the Regt. 1 Dec. 1708.

²⁹ Comn. not forthcoming. Out of the Regt. in 1708.

³⁰ Comn. not forthcoming. 1st Lieut. of the Grendr. Cy. 23 Apr. 1705. Served throughout Marlborough's campaigns.

³¹ Ens. in above Regt. before July 1702. £22 bounty money to his widow.

³² Comn. not forthcoming. £22 bounty money to his widow.

³³ Comn. not forthcoming.

³⁴ and ³⁵ Untraced. Comns. not forthcoming.

³⁶ Appointed Chaplain to above Regt. before 7 July 1702. Served at Ramillies. Left the Regt. 1 Dec 1708.

³⁷ Untraced. Appointed Adjt. subsequent to 7 July 1702. Out of the Regt. in 1708.

³⁸ Comn. not forthcoming. Out of the Regt in 1708.

³⁹ Appointed subsequent to 7 July 1702. Out of the Regt. 28 July 1706.

⁴⁰ Untraced.

THE BLENHEIM ROLL.

BRIGADIER-GENERAL MEREDYTH'S REGT. OF FOOT.*

	£	s.	d.	
COLONEL.				
[Tho.] Meredyth, W. - - -	144	0	0	Bounty.
LIEUT.-COLONEL COMMANDING.				
[Tho.] Bellew¹ - - - -	51	0	0	,,
MAJOR.				
[Tho.] Buckeridge² - - -	45	0	0	,,
CAPTAINS.				
Jas. Browning³ - - - -	30	0	0	,,
Jas. Douglas⁴ - - - -	30	0	0	,,
Phil. Fletcher⁵ - - - -	30	0	0	,,
[Hen.] Meredyth⁶ - - -	30	0	0	,,
Robt. Mundy⁷ - - - -	30	0	0	,,
Ric. Carthy⁸ - - - -	30	0	0	,,
[Jas.] Butler⁹ - - - -	30	0	0	,,
CAPT-LIEUT.				
Toby Cremer¹⁰ - - - -	14	0	0	,,
LIEUTENANTS.				
Tho. Timpson¹¹ - - - -	14	0	0	,,
Tho. Bennet¹² - - - -	14	0	0	,,
Tho. Jones¹³ - - - -	14	0	0	,,
Jno. Sotheby,¹⁴ W. - - -	28	0	0	,,
[Fred.] Edmonds,¹⁵ W. - -	28	0	0	,,
Jno. Cairnes,¹⁶ W. - - -	28	0	0	,,
Roger Nield,¹⁷ W. - - -	28	0	0	,,
Henry Byron,¹⁸ W. - - -	28	0	0	,,
[Wm. Cornwall,¹⁹ K.]				
[Ric. Baukham, Lieut. and Adjt.²⁰ K.]				
ENSIGNS.				
Chas. Stedman²¹ - - - -	11	0	0	,,
Adam Loftus²² - - - -	11	0	0	,,
Ralph Walsh,²³ W. - - -	22	0	0	,,
Robt. Annesley,²⁴ W. - -	22	0	0	,,
Paul Wood,²⁵ W. - - -	22	0	0	,,
Chas. Ogilby,²⁶ W. - - -	22	0	0	,,
Jas. Kent,²⁷ W. - - -	22	0	0	,,
[—— Billing,²⁸ K.]				
[—— Jackson,²⁹ K.]				
QR.-MR.				
Jno. Nangle³⁰ - - - -	14	0	0	,,
SURGEON.				
Adam Williamson³¹ - - -	12	0	0	,,
SURGEON'S MATE.				
Tho. Bell³² - - - -	7	10	0	,,

* The 37th Foot. When territorial titles were first bestowed on British Regiments in 1751, the above corps was styled the "North Hampshire Regt.," but it was really raised in Ireland, as appears from the following notice in the *Dublin Flying Post*, 2-4 May 1702:—"Drums beat up daily in this city for soldiers for Col. Coote's and Colonel Meredith's Regts., which are raising here."

The non-commissioned officers and men who received bounty money were 29 sergeants, each of whom received £2; 34 corporals, each of whom received £1 10s.; and 480 privates (including drummers), each of whom received £1. At Schellenberg 1 sergeant was killed and 3 wounded; 18 privates were killed and 57 wounded.

[1] Appointed Capt. in Visct. Charlemont's Regt. of Foot 12 June 1696. Placed on half-pay in 1698. Re-appointed Capt. in Lord Charlemont's newly-raised Regt. of Foot 28 June 1701. Under date of 24 Dec. 1700, Luttrell has this entry in his *Diary*:—" Saturday morning Major-General Stewart and Captain Bellew (whose right hands were both disabled in the late war) fought on foot with pistols; the first fired, being within 2 yards of the other, and shot him through the hat, whereupon Bellew generously threw away his pistol, saying he did not desire to kill him" (Vol. IV. p. 721). Appointed Major of Col. Tho. Meredyth's Regt. of Foot 13 Feb. 1702. In a memorial to the Rt. Hon. Robt. Harley, dated 28 Feb. 1710, this officer enumerates his war services as follows:—" Served at the first siege of Limerick as a Captain. Was in the Brest expedition and at the burning of Dieppe. Commanded Brigadier Meredith's Regt. at Blenheim. Was at the siege of Palamos in Catalonia, and served 2 campaigns at sea. Made Lieut.-Colonel of Militia Dragoons in Dublin County when a Jacobite invasion was threatened." *Treasury Papers*, Vol. CXXXII., No. 19.

[2] Appointed Capt. of the Grendr. Cy. in Col. Jno. Courthope's Regt. of Foot in Ireland 23 Apr. 1694. Capt. in Col. Tho. Meredyth's Regt. of Foot 13 Feb. 1702. Major before 1704. Out of the Regt. 6 Nov. 1708.

[3] Appointed Capt. in above Regt. 13 Feb. 1702. Out of the Regt. in 1708. In 1706 this officer applied to Marlborough for a Major's Comn. in the New Levies—" Was one of the first that appeared in arms at Inniskilling, in Ireland, in 1688, and served all that war as Capt. of Grenadiers in Col. Hamilton's, aftds. Col. Creighton's Regt., and was at the storming of both the towns of Athlone" (*War Office MS.*). Out of the Army in 1710.

[4] Appointed Capt. in above Regt. 13 Feb. 1702. Major of Col. Owen Wynne's newly-raised Regt. of Foot 25 Mar. 1705. Exchanged to Brigdr.-Gen. Ric. Sutton's Regt. of Foot as Lt.-Col. 2 Apr. 1712. Placed on half-pay in 1713.

[5] Son of Richard Fletcher and ancestor of Sir Hen. Fletcher, Bart., of Clea Hall, Cumberland. Appointed Capt. in Sir Ric. Atkins's Regt. of Foot 23 Apr. 1694. Capt. in Col. Tho. Meredyth's Regt. of Foot 13 Feb. 1702. Bt.-Major 1 Jan. 1707. Major 6 Nov. 1708. Served in several of Marlborough's campaigns and retired by the sale of his Comn. in July 1710 (*Marlborough Dispatches*, Vol. V., p. 67). D. in 1744 at a very advanced age. See Burke's *Baronetage*.

[6] 2nd son of Chas. Meredyth of Newtown, Co. Meath. Comn. in above Regt. not forthcoming. Applied for a Lt.-Colonelcy in the New Levies in 1706, and was appointed Lt.-Col. of Col. Tho. Stanwix's Regt. of Foot 12 Apr. 1706. Out of last-named Regt. in 1712.

[7] Appointed Capt. in Col. Ric. Brewer's Regt of Foot 1 Feb. 1697. Capt. in Col. Tho. Meredyth's Regt. of Foot 13 Feb. 1702. Major of Col. Edm. Soames's Regt. of Foot 25 March 1705. Out of last-named Regt. in 1708.

[8] Appointed Capt.-Lieut. of Col. Tho. Meredyth's Regt. of Foot 13 Feb. 1702. Capt.'s Comn. not forthcoming. Served throughout Marlborough's campaigns.

[9] Possibly of the Belturbet family, Co. Cavan, one of whom md. Lt.-Col. Hen. Meredyth. Appointed Capt. in above Regt. 1 March 1704. Major of above Regt. in 1717.

[10] Appointed Lieut. in Col. Tho. Meredyth's Regt. of Foot 13 Feb. 1702. Capt. 25 March 1705. Served at Malplaquet. Brigade-Major to the Forces sent to Canada under Brigdr.-Gen. Jno. Hill 1 March 1711. Capt. in Col. Clayton's Regt. of Foot 18 Oct. 1711. Commandant of the Risbank (*sic*) at Dunkirk 27 June 1712. Placed on half-pay in 1713. Restored to full pay as Capt. in Col. Hen. Harrison's Regt. of Foot in 1716. Capt. and Lt.-Col. in the 3rd Foot Guards 25 Dec. 1717. 2nd Major in 3rd Foot Guards 19 July 1736. D. in 1739.

[11] Appointed Lieut. in above Regt. 13 Feb. 1702. Served several campaigns under Marlborough who recommended this officer to the Queen's favour, in Feb. 1710, for the post of " a poor knight of Windsor" (*Marlborough Dispatches*, Vol. IV., p. 688).

[12] Appointed Lieut. in above Regt. 13 Feb. 1702. Was recommended for a Cy. in the New Levies, in 1706, by Brigadier Meredyth, who stated that this officer "had served 17 years as a Lieutenant" (*War Office MS.*). Appointed Capt. in Lord Paston's Regt. of Foot in 1706. Placed on half-pay in 1712.

[13] Appointed Ens. in above Regt. 13 Feb. 1702. Lieut. 1 March 1704. Served throughout Marlborough's campaigns.

[14] Lieut.'s Comn. in above Regt. not forthcoming. Wounded at Schellenberg. Capt. 24 March 1706. Served throughout Marlborough's campaigns.

[15] Appointed 2nd Lieut. of the Grendr. Cy. in above Regt. 13 Feb. 1702. In 1706 this officer gave the following account of his services when applying to Marlborough for a Comn. in the New Levies: " Has served the Crown 17 years, and particularly as Captain in the siege of Londonderry and in all the wars of Ireland where he raised, armed, and subsisted a Company at his own charge, several weeks, whereby he suffered very great losses. He has likewise ridd (*sic*) nine years in the 2nd troop of Guards, and is now first Lieut. of Grenadiers in Brigadier Meredyth's Regt., and the second eldest Lieut. in the Regt. Prays to be preferred in the Horse, Foot, or Dragoons" (*War Office MS.*). Out of Meredyth's Regt. in 1708.

[16] Appointed Lieut. in above Regt. 13 Feb. 1702. Wounded at both Schellenberg and Blenheim. Capt. in Col. Wm. Breton's Regt. of Foot 8 Sept. 1710. Placed on half-pay in 1713.

[17] Appointed Ens. in above Regt. 13 Feb. 1702. Wounded at Schellenberg. Lieut.'s Comn. not forthcoming. Out of the Regt. in 1708.

[18] Appointed Ens. in above Regt. 13 Feb. 1702. Lieut.'s Comn. not forthcoming. Wounded at both Schellenberg and Blenheim. Capt.-Lieut. 25 June 1705. Adjt. 11 March 1708. Capt. 6 Nov. 1708. Served throughout Marlborough's campaigns.

[19] Appointed Ens. in above Regt. 13 Feb. 1702. Lieut.'s Comn. not forthcoming. Killed at Schellenberg. £28 bounty money to his widow.

[20] Appointed Adjt. to Sir Ric. Atkins's Regt. of Foot 29 Jan. 1696. Lieut. and Adjt. to Col. Meredyth's Regt. before 1704. Wounded at Schellenberg. £40 bounty money to his widow.

[21] Appointed Ens. in above Regt. 13 Feb. 1702. 1st Lieut. of the Grendr. Cy. 25 June 1704 (sic). Served throughout Marlborough's campaigns.

[22] A direct descendant of Dr. Adam Loftus, Archbishop of Armagh, temp. Queen Elizabeth. Appointed Ens. to Brigadier Meredyth's own Cy. in above Regt. 25 June 1704. Lieut. 11 March 1708. Served throughout Marlborough's campaigns.

[23] Appointed Ens. in above Regt. 13 Feb. 1702. Lieut.'s Comn. not forthcoming. Wounded at Schellenberg. Capt. 25 March 1707. Served at Malplaquet.

[24] Comn. not forthcoming. Wounded at Schellenberg. Out of the Regt. in 1708.

[25] Comn. not forthcoming. Wounded at Schellenberg. Lieut. 22 July 1706. Serving as Qr.-Mr. in above Regt. in 1709.

[26] Appointed Ens. to Col. Meredyth's own Cy. in above Regt. 25 March 1703. Wounded at Schellenberg. Lieut. 25 June 1705. Served at Malplaquet.

[27] Appointed Ens. in above Regt. 25 June 1704. Wounded at Schellenberg. Lieut. 29 June 1708. Served at Malplaquet.

[28] and [29] Killed at Schellenberg. Comns. and Christian names not forthcoming.

[30] Comn. not forthcoming. Appointed Lieut. in above Regt. 27 March 1708. Served at Malplaquet.

[31] Comn. not forthcoming. Serving in above Regt. in 1709.

[32] Possibly the "Thos. Ball" appointed Surgeon to Lord Cutts's Regt. of Dragoons in Ireland in 1706.

LIST OF THE WIDOWS OR CHILDREN OF THE SLAIN OFFICERS OF THE REGIMENTS AFORE-MENTIONED.

Regts.	Quality of the Officers.	Widows.	Children.	Allowance. £
[Staff]	Brigadier-General Row	—	[2]	90
Wood	Lieut.-Colonel	Mrs. Featherstonhalgh	—	177
,,	Captain	Mrs. Carrington	2	129
,,	Cornet	Mrs. Odiarne	2	84
Cadogan	Lieutenant	Mrs. Grueber	—	90
Wyndham	Major	Mrs. Chenevix	3	162
,,	Lieutenant	Mrs. Payne	4	90
,,	Cornet and Adjt.	Mrs. Thomson	2	114
Schomberg	Lieutenant	Mrs. Hawks	3	90
,,	Quartermaster	Mrs. Kelsall	2	51
,,	Quartermaster	Mrs. Charlton	—	51
Hay	Captain	Mrs. Young	2	93
Orkney	Lieut.-Colonel	Mrs. White	2	102
,,	Captain	Mrs. Bayly	2	60
,,	Captain	Mrs. Murray	1	60
,,	Lieutenant	Mrs. Moor	5	28
,,	Lieutenant	Mrs. Kerr	2	28
Churchill	Lieutenant	Mrs. Palfrey	4	28
North and Grey	Captain	Lady Sands	—	60
,,	Captain	Mrs. Cunningham	—	60
,,	Captain Dawes	—	1	60
,,	Captain	Mrs. Astley	—	60
,,	Lieutenant	Mrs. Hornby	2	28
,,	Lieutenant	Mrs. Weekes	—	28
Howe	Captain	Mrs. Tancred	1	60
,,	Lieutenant	Mrs. King	4	28
,,	Lieutenant	Mrs. Kerr	1	28
,,	Ensign	Mrs. Jackson	4	22
Derby	Major	Mrs. Morden	—	90
,,	Ensign	Mrs. Gordon	3	22
,,	Surgeon	Mrs. Whitfield	—	24
Hamilton	Captain	Mrs. Brown	3	60
,,	Captain	Mrs. Rolleston	—	60
Mordaunt	Col. Row	—	2	144
,,	Lieut.-Colonel	Mrs. Dalyell	2	102
,,	Lieut.-Colonel	Mrs. Campbell	—	102
,,	Lieutenant	Mrs. Vandergracht	2	28
,,	Lieutenant	Mrs. Campbell	—	28
Ingoldsby	Lieutenant	Mrs. Ogilvie	1	28
,,	Lieutenant	Mrs. Egan	3	28
,,	Lieutenant	Mrs. Fraser	5	28
,,	2nd Lieutenant	Mrs. Rowlands	3	22
Tatton	Captain Tichborne	—	3	60
,,	Captain	Mrs. Gardiner	—	60
,,	Captain	Mrs. Fitz Symonds	—	60
,,	Lieutenant	Mrs. Parrot	3	28
Ferguson	Lieutenant	Mrs. Seton	3	28
,,	Lieutenant	Mrs. Moncreif	1	28
,,	Ensign	Mrs. Bernard	—	22
,,	Ensign	Mrs. Hay	—	22
Meredyth	Lieutenant and Adjt.	Mrs. Baukham	—	40
,,	Lieutenant	Mrs. Cornwall	—	28

THE BLENHEIM ROLL.

Addition which his Grace the Duke of Marlborough is pleased to make to this List of his proportion of the bounty money, to be disposed of as shall be hereafter directed, vizt. :—

		£		
As Captain-General of Her Majesty's Forces	- - - -	600		
[Widows and Children] - - - - - - - -		3,013		
Total of the General Officers, Regiments, &c., brought forward -		42,108		
		£45,721		

Abstract of the distribution of the Prize Money :—

		s.	d.
General Officers, &c., [and Staff] - - - -	£4,142	7	6
Train of Artillery - - - - - - -	1,608	10	0
Hospital - - - - - - - - -	435	0	0
Disabled men - - - - - - - -	4,000	0	0
	£10,185	17	6
Five Regts. of Horse - - - - - -	8,813	10	0
Two Regts. of Dragoons - - - - - -	2,684	0	0
Fourteen Battalions of Foot - - - - -	20,424	12	6
Widows - - - - - - - - -	3,013	0	0
	£45,121	0	0
For horses of the English Horse and Dragoons dead of the distemper abroad, and for arms and accoutrements lost in the late actions in Germany - -	£13,292	0	0
For making good the arms and accoutrements of the Foot, lost in the said action, £400 to each of the 14 Battalions - - - - - - - -	5,600	0	0
	£18,892	0	0
	45,121	0	0
	£64,013	0	0
	Remains 987	0	0
	Total £65,000	0	0

This account has been prepared by order of his Grace the Duke of Marlborough, with the advice of the General Officers in pursuance of a letter from the Most Hon. the Lord High Treasurer of England of the 10 Feb. 1704/5, desiring his Grace to consider in what manner the Royal Bounty her Majesty is pleased to bestow might be most usefully applied to the officers and soldiers of those Regiments that were in Germany, for the better enabling the said Regiments to take the field, as also for the widows of the officers and soldiers that were slain in the actions there, with particular regard to the maimed and wounded soldiers, and what may be allowed thereout towards their future support.

H. St. John.

March the 6th 1704/5.

INDEX.

A

Abercrombie, Jas., 2, 33.
Abercromby, Alex., 27.
Abington, Ric., 39.
Adams, Jas., 42.
........., Mat., 29.
Agnew, And., 24.
Aikman, Jas., 66.
Albritton, Thos., 63.
Aldy, Wm., 60.
Alexander, Chas., 13.
Amyand, Claud, 12.
Annesley, Robt., 69.
Ansley, Robt. *See supra.*
Armstrong, And., 48.
........., Geo., 24.
........., Jno., 8.
........., Phil., 16.
........., Thos., 16.
Arthur, Alex., 40.
Arwaker, Edm. *See* Earwaker.
Ashby, Wm., 2, 16.
Astley, Chas., 45, 72.
Ayloffe, Jno., 51.

B

Babbe, Simon. *See infra.*
Babe, Simon, 27.
Badenoch, Jno., 57.
Baily, Jno., 36, 72.
Baker, Geo., 20.
Balfour, (—), 66.
........., Jno., 42.
Ball, Chas., 8.
Ballantine, Jas., 33.
Ballard, Jno., 63.
Bannerman, Jno., 36.
Barker, Ric., 60.
Barrell, Wm., 29, 30.
Barton, (—), 42.
........., Robt., 48.
........., Roger, 13.

Baukham, Ric., 69, 72.
Bayly, Edm., 60.
........., Jno., 63.
Bayne, Roderick, 51.
Bean, Roderick. *See supra.*
Beatty, Chas., 27.
Bell, Thos., 69.
Bellew, Thos., 69.
Benbow, Wm., 13.
Bennet, Thos., 69.
Berkeley, Hen., 63.
Bernard, Mat., 66.
........., Pat., 66, 72.
Beswick, Ric., 20.
Bibby, Jno., 30.
Billing, (—), 69.
Billingsley, Chas., 48.
........., Chris., 13.
Bishop, Ben., 13.
Bisset, Jas., 33.
Black, Jas., 33.
Blackader, Jno., 66.
Blakeney, Jno., 54.
........., Wm., 54 *bis.*
Blood, Holcroft, 8.
Blount, Chas., 8.
........., Hen., 29.
Bodil, J—, 34.
Boisragon, Dan., 27.
Bolton, Jas., 39.
........., Ric., 48.
Bonell, And., 8.
Borthwick, Hen., 66.
........., Wm., 66.
Boullay, Peter, 34.
Bourden, Jno., 8.
Bousfield, Wm., 8.
Boyd, Ninian, 24.
Boyer, Pet., 22.
Bozier, Jno., 42.
Bragg, Phil., 29.
Breams, Walt., 45.
Breton, Wm., 48.
Bright, Dan., 63.
Bringfield, Jas., 2.
Brisbane, Wm., 36.
Briscoe, Chris., 8.
Brown, (—), 27.
........., Geo., 33.
........., Hen., 54, 72.

Browne, Hen., 29.
........., Randal, 51.
Browning, Jas., 69.
Brownjohn, Fras., 57.
Bruce, Thos., 36.
Buckeridge, Thos., 69.
Buller, Sam., 45 *bis*.
Burton, Constantine, 45.
........., Jno., 63.
........., Thos., 45.
Butler, Jas., 69.
Byron, Hen., 69.

C

Cabrol, Dan., 18.
Cadogan, Wm., 1 *bis*, 18.
Cadroy, Steph., 60.
Cairnes, Jno., 69.
Calder, Jno., 48.
Caldicot (—), 39.
Caldwell, Hugh, 2, 27.
Campbell, Alex., 66.
........., Jas., 57.
........., Jno., 57, 72.
........., Wm., 57, 72.
Campion, (—), 39.
........., Rowland, 29.
Cardonnel, Adam, 1.
Carnac, Pet., 63.
Carr, Thos. *See* Kerr.
........., Wm. *See* Kerr.
........., Wm., 42.
Carrey (*sic*), Jno., 8.
Carrick, Wm., 60.
Carrington, Chas., 16, 72.
Carthy, Ric., 69.
Cator, Roger, 42.
Cavendish, Geo., 45.
Chambers, Jas., 43.
Chapman, (—), 16.
Charlton, (—), 22, 72.
........., (—), 51.
Chaytor, Hen., 8.
Chenevix, Phil., 20, 72.
Cherry, Jno., 54.
Chester, Granada, 29.
Child, Geo., 16.
Chivers, Jno., 39.
Churchill, General Chas., 1, 39.
........., Lt.-Col. Chas., 2, 39.
Clarke, Jno., 22.
Clavers, Hen., 42.
Cockburn, Chas., 33.
Cocksedge, Wm., 27.

Coghlan, Garret, 51.
Colombière, Ant., 42.
Colson, Ben., 22.
Colville, Arch., 33.
Congreve, Ralph, 42.
........., Wm., 42.
Conway (or McConway), Geo., 36.
Cooke, Thos., 51.
Cookman, Hen., 60.
Coote, Ric., 22.
Cornewall, Wm. (or Cornwall), 69, 72.
Cornwallis, Fred., 48.
Craig, Jas., 33.
Cranston, Jas., 66.
Crauford, Jno., 57.
........., Wm., 24.
Creamer, Toby. *See infra*.
Cremer, Toby, 69.
Creed, Ric., 22.
Crispin, Dan., 18.
Crocker, (—), 20.
Crosby, Jno., 18.
Crowther, Thos., 13.
Croye, Dan., 45.
........., Peter, 45.
Cruseau, Jno., 22.
Cuningham, Jno., 45, 72.
Cunningham, David, 33.
........., Jas., 33.
Cuttle, Ben., 42, 43.
Cutts, Jno., Lord, 1.

D

Dalrymple, Jno., 66.
Dalyell, Jno., 57, 72.
Daniel, Wm., 45.
Davis, (—), 63.
Dawes, Warner, 45, 72.
Dawson, (—), 48.
........., Jas., 51.
........., Thos., 45.
Dean, (—), 48.
Deane, Jno., 13.
........., Ric., 22.
........., Theophilus, 12.
Debize, David, 46.
De Cone, Pet. *See infra*.
De Cosne, Pet., 42.
De Culant, Jeffrey, 29.
De Faure, Fras., 48.
De Montresor, Jas., 57.
De Monty, Sam., 34.
De Sibourg, Chas., 22.
Dickenson, Dan., 48.
Dickson, Jas., 36.
........., Pat., 66.

Dillington, Tristram, 13.
Disney, Hen., 2, 39.
Dobbins, Jas., 63.
Dodsworth, Ant., 13.
........., Jno., 13.
D'Offranville, Peter, 54.
Dormer, Fleetwood, 60.
........., Jas., 29.
........., Phil., 29.
Douglas, Arch., 66.
........., Geo., 66.
........., Capt. Jas., 69.
........., Qr.-Mr. Jas., 24.
........., 1st Lieut. Jas., 57.
........., 1st Lieut. Jno., 57.
........., Ens. Jno., 63.
........., Wm., 24.
Dove, Thos., 16.
Drummond, Thos., 66.
........., Wm., 66.
Drury, Robt., 27.
Dudgeon, Jas., 24.
Dunbar, Jno., (Rl. Irish Dragoons), 27.
........., Jno., (Rl. Scots Fusiliers), 57.
........., Ric., 27.
Dunbreck, Chas., 57.
Duran, Adriel, 34.
Durel, Hen., 2.

E

Earwaker, Edm., 54.
Edmonds, Fred., 69.
........., Ric., 20.
Edwards, Arth., 48.
Egan, Constantine, 60, 72.
Elliot, (—), 36.
........., Wm., 57.
Erskine, Harry, 57.
........., Jno., 36.
Evans, Owen, 40.
Eyme, Isaac, 60.
Eyton, Jas., 2, 16.

F

Fairlie, Alex., 57.
Falconer, Robt., 57.
Farcey, Jno., 42.
Farrer, Jas., 18.
Featherstonhalgh, Jno., 16, 72.
Ferguson, Jas., 1, 66.
........., Jno., 66.
........., Leonard, 66.
........., Robt., 66.

Ferrers, Thos., 29.
Fielding, Edm., 42.
Finch, Jno., 63.
Finley, Wm., 20.
Fitz Simons, Vere, 63, 72.
Fleming, Jas., 18.
........., Mich., 51.
Fletcher, Geo., 18.
........., Hen., 42.
........., Jno., 8.
........., Phil., 69.
Forbes, Alex., 8.
........., Arthur, Lord, 36.
Forrest, (—), 66.
Forrester, Fras., 16.
Fowke, Jno., (or Foulke), 48.
Fraine, And., 24.
Franks, Godfrey, 8.
Fraser, Alex., 60, 72.
French, Edw., 8.
Frere, Jer. (or Freyer), 45.
Fullerton, Jas., 60.
Furnesse, Sam., 63.
Fury, Jas. (?), 2.

G

Gaile, Jno., 18.
Gardiner, Jno., 63.
........., Pat., 51.
........., Surgeon-Genl. Thos., 2.
........., Capt. Thos., 63, 72.
Garston, Jno., 18.
........., Thos., 48.
Gatford, Jno., 20.
Gay, (—), 45.
Gelmuyden, Pet., 8.
Geneste, Wm., 12.
Gibson, Jno., 12.
Gilman, Stephen, 54.
Girle, Jno., 9.
Gittings, Nathaniel, 39.
Godfrey, Fras, 29.
Goldie, Jno., 12.
Gooch, Wm., 51.
Goodwin, Jas., 16.
........., Wm., 13.
Gordon, (—). *See* Gordon, Pat.
........., Alex., 33.
........., Hen., 57.
........., Jno. (Rl. Regt. of Foot), 36.
........., Jno. (Earl of Derby's Regt. of Foot), 51, 72.
........., Pat., 2, 36.
Gore, Ric., 27.
Goudet, Joachim, 42.

Graham, Jas., 36.
........., Metcalf, 18.
Grant, Alex., 24.
........., Peter, 39.
Granville, Jno., 45.
Green, Geo., 45.
Grierson, And., 12.
........., Jno., 39.
Groffey, Peter, 63.
Groves, Hen., 45.
Grueber, Jno. Hen., 18, 72.
Guybons, Robt., 8.
Guyon, Wm., 20.

H

Hadden, Geo., 36.
Hall, Chas., 20.
........., Geo., 54.
Halliday, Wm., 48 *bis*.
Hallman, Nich., 13.
Hamilton, Alex., 36.
........., And., 36.
........., Arch., 33 *bis*.
........., Edwd., 2, 27.
........., Fred., 1, 54.
........., Hans, 51.
........., Jas., 27.
........., Robt., 36.
Hamars, Pet. *See infra*.
Hammers, Pet., 42.
Hara, Alex. *See* O'Hara.
Hare, Fras., 1.
Hargrave, Edwd., 48.
Harraway, Chas., 36.
Harris, Archdale, 30.
Harrison, (—), 60.
........., Hen., 48 *bis*.
........., Jas., 20.
........., Thos., 39.
Hartwell, Geo., 13.
Harvey, Jno., 54.
........., Sam., 51.
Hastings, Ant., 29.
Hawkes, Sam., 22, 72.
Hawkins, Fras., 8.
Hawtayne, Wm., 60.
Hay, Jno., 66, 72.
........., Lord Jno., 24.
........., Theodore, 36.
Hellowes, Jno., 45.
Heming, Ric., 60.
Herbert, Caleb, 48.
Hesketh, Jas., 51.
........., Thos., 51.
Hetley, Jno., 39.

Hicks, Thos., 16.
Highmes, Fras. Sydney, 29.
Hill, (—), 57.
........., Jno., 27.
........., Maurice, 24.
Hobart, Jas., 42.
Holliday, Wm. *See* Halliday.
Holman, Thos., 8.
Hooke, Thos., 51.
........., Wm., 51.
Hopeke, Jno. Hen., 8.
Hornby, Arth., 45, 72.
Horne, Alex., 51.
Howard, Jas., 29.
Hudson, Jno., 12.
Hull, Thos., 16.
Hume, Alex., 33.
........., Jas., 33.
Hunter, Jno., 27.
........., Robt., 27.
Hussey, Nat., 54.

I

Illingworth, Robt., 51.
Inglis, Surgeon Alex., 14.
........., Ens. Alex., 36.
........., Geo., 36.
Ingoldsby, Jas., 60.
........., Ric., 1, 60.
Innes, Walt., 36.
Innis, Alex. *See* Inglis.
Irwin, Alex., 2, 33.

J

Jackson, (—), 69.
........., Jno., 51.
........., Cornet Thos., 13.
........., Ensign Thos., 48, 72.
Jenkins, Newce (*sic*), 60.
Jefferson, Jno., 29.
Jeoffreyson, Jno. *See supra*.
Jevereau, Isaac, 2, 60.
Johnson, Robt, 48.
Johnston, Jno., 27.
........., Ric., 27.
........., Sam., 57.
Jones, Jas., 60.
........., Griffith, 60.
........., Thos., 69.
Juckes, Edwd., 48.

INDEX.

K

Kane, Florence, 57.
........., Ric., 54.
Kaye, Jno., 51.
Keith, Gideon, 24.
Kelsall, (—), 22, 72.
Kenny, Wm., 39.
Kent, Jas., 69.
Kerr, Robt., 33.
........., Thos., 36, 72.
........., Wm. (Brigdr. Gen. Howe's Regt. of Foot), 48, 72.
........., Wm. (Rl. Regt. of Foot), 36.
........., Wm. (or Carr), 42.
Kidd, And., 33.
King, Ric., 8.
........., Wm., 48, 72.
Kingston, Fras., 13, 14.
Kygo, Jas., 57.
Kyrle, Wm., 20.

L

La Chapelle, (—), 16.
Lacoude, Jno., 63.
Lancaster, Wm. (?), 63.
Lane, Wm., 45.
La Penotière, Fred., 54.
Lascelles, Ric., 48.
........., Thos., 8.
Lauder, Geo., 24.
Laughlin, Thos., 54.
Law, Chas., 13.
........., Nathaniel, 13.
........., Pet., 2, 13.
Lawrence, David, 16.
........., Dr. Thos., 1, 12.
Lawson, Jas., 66.
Leathes, Moses, 54.
........., Wm., 54.
Lee, Robt., 12.
Legg, Chas., 45.
........., Ric., 48.
Le Roy, Chas., 22.
Leslie, Lachlan, 48.
........., Jas., 48.
Lewis, Paul, 42.
Ligas, J—, 34.
Ligonier, Jno., 45.
Lilly, Jas., 54.
Lindsay, Fras., 66.
........., Jas., 36.

Lindsey, Jas. *See* Lindsay.
Lisle, Pat., 13.
........., Wm. *See* Lyall.
Little, Arch., 22.
Livingston, Alex., 66.
........., Jas. (Scots Greys), 24.
........., Jas. (Rl. Regt. of Foot), 36.
Lloyd, Leond., 42 *bis*.
........., Verney, 42.
........., Wm., 2, 39.
Loftus, Adam, 69.
Looker, Jno., 22.
Low, (—), 66.
Lowick, Jno. 20.
Lowndes, Chas., 43.
Luke, Oliver, 39.
Lumley, Hen., 1, 13.
Lyall, Wm., 36.
Lyth, Robt., 22.

M

McConway, Geo. (or Conway), 36.
McDougal, (—), 33.
McHenry, Wm., 57.
McIlroy, (—), 33.
Mackean, Geo., 27.
Mackenzie, Duncan, 36.
Mackreth, Wm., 51.
Maclean, Chas., 66.
Macmahon, Jno., 18 *bis*.
McQueen, Jno., 36.
Magennis, Hugh, 16.
Mallard, Thos., 24.
Mallery, Fras., 63.
Mann, (—), 67.
Marlborough, John Churchill, Duke of, 1, 29.
Marshall, (—), 66.
Marwood, Thos., 8.
Mason, Chas., 42.
Mathews, Ric., 60.
Maturin, Peter, 63.
Maxwell, Pat., 57.
Meade, Pat., 63.
Melvill, Jno., 39.
........., Robt., 39.
........., Wm., 36 *bis*.
Meoles, Jno., 39.
Meredyth, Hen., 69.
........., Thos., 1 *bis*, 69.
Middleton, Wm., 45.
Molesworth, Ric., 33.
Moncreif, Hen., 66, 72.
Monroe, And., 66.

Montgomery, Hugh, 39.
........., Wm., 36.
Montresor. *See* De Montresor.
Moor, Jas., 36.
........., Wm., 33, 72.
Mordaunt, Jno., Lord, 29.
Morden, Jno. (or Mordaunt), 51, 72.
Morey, Jno., 13.
Morgan, Geo., 2, 60.
Morinier, Pat. (or Peter), 33.
Morris, Geo., 48.
Morton, Jno., 42.
Moyle, Jno., 54.
........., Wm., 54.
Muirhead, Wm., 36.
Mundy, Robt., 69.
Munden, Ric., 29.
Munt (*sic*), John, 16.
Murray, (—), 36.
........., Edwd., 36.
........., Ens. Jno. (Royal Regt. of Foot), 33.
........., Capt. Jno. (do.   ), 33, 72.

N

Nangle, Jno., 69.
Napier, Fras., 42.
........., Robt., 18.
Neilson, Wm., 12.
Newell, Thos, 20.
Nicholetts, Gilb., 29.
Nield, Roger, 69.
Nisbet, Jas., 24.
North and Grey, Wm., Lord, 45.
Norton, Robt., 22.
Noyes, Sam., 33.

O

Odiarne, Chas., 16, 72.
Ogilby, Chas., 69.
Ogilvie, Alex., 66.
........., Geo., 33.
........., Jas., 57.
Ogilvy, (—), 60, 72.
Ogle, Nathaniel, 12.
Oglethorpe, Lewis, 2.
O'Hara, Alex., 8.
Oldfield, Somerford, 16.
........., Thos., 63.
Oliphant, (—), 12.
........., Pat., 66.
Orr, Wm., 12.
Orkney, Geo. Hamilton, Earl of, 1, 33.

P

Palfrey, Geo., 39, 72.
Palmer, Wm., 13.
Palmes, Fras., 1, 20.
........., Steph., 22.
Panton, Thos., 2, 13.
Parke, Dan., 2.
Parker, Robt., 54.
Parr, Jno., 63.
Parrot, Jno., 63, 72.
Paterson, Jno., 60.
Patrickson, Ric., 48.
Pawlet, Jno., 9.
Payne, Wm., 20, 72.
Peacock, Nich., 60.
Pearson, Ben., 36.
Pendlebury, Jas., 8.
Pennefather, Mat., 2, 60.
Penotière, Fred. *See* La Penotière.
Petry, Jno., 20.
Peyton, Hen., 39.
Pickering, Jno., 29.
Pierson, Ric., 29.
Pigot, Southwell, 60.
Pinsent, Jas., 54.
Pitt, (—), 2.
........., Jno., 16.
........., Mat., 14.
Pitcairn, David, 66.
Pocock, Jno., 29.
Poé, Jas., 27.
Poilblanc, Hen., 45.
Pollexfen, Thos., 63.
Pope, Ric., 22.
Powell, Geo., 42.
........., Jno., 60.
Preston, Chas., 24.
........., Geo., 24.
........., Jno., 39.
........., Thos, 45, 46.
Price, Edwd., 60.
Prime, Phil., 22.
Primrose, Gilb., 29.
........., Wm., 57.
Pujolas, Ant., 2, 29.
........., St. Denis, 29.
Pyne, Thos., 39.

R

Raleigh, Granville, 45.
........., Walt., 29.
Ramsay, Jno., 63.
........., Lewis, 42.
........., Ralph, 63.

INDEX.

Ray, Jno., 63.
Reddich, Jno. 51.
........., Ric., 51.
Reeves, Jno., 22.
........., Valentine, 29.
Renton, Alex., 57.
Reynolds, Hen., 54.
Ribier, Gideon, 45.
Ribton, Peter, 42.
Rich, Robt., 29.
Richards, Chas., 60.
Ricketts, (—), 16.
Roberts, Sam., 54.
Robertson, Pat., 24.
Robinson, Geo., 20.
........., Molineux, 22.
Roddam, Robt., 12.
Rolleston, Arphaxad, 54, 72.
........., Wm., 54.
Ross, Alex., 33.
........., Chas., 1, 27.
........., David, 27 *bis*.
Rossington, Jno., 45.
........., Robt., 45.
Row, Arch., 1, 57, 72.
Rowlands, Reg., 60, 72.
Ryves, Val. *See* Reeves.

S

Sabine, Joseph, 60.
........., Whitfield, 60.
........., Wm., 51.
Sandby, Jno., 39.
Sandilands, Walt., 48.
Sands, Sir Jno., 45, 72.
Saunders, Ric., 20.
Savage, (—), 42.
Scaife, Thos., 20.
Scawen, Fras. (?), 2.
Scott, Hugh, 39.
........., Jas. (Royal Scots Greys), 24.
........., Jas. (Lord North and Grey's Regt.), 45.
........., Qr.-Mr. Jno., 13.
........., Lieut. Jno., 39.
........., Wm., 30.
Scrimshire, Alex., 39 *bis*.
Seton, Geo., 66, 72.
Seymour, Jno., 33.
Shairp, Walt., 57.
Shaw, Wm., 13.
Shute, Sam., 16.
Sibourg, Chas. de. *See* De Sibourg.
Simonds, Thos., 48.
Simpson, Jas., 66.

Sinclair, Geo., 48.
Skene, Geo., 24.
Skelston, Jno., 27.
Slaughter, Jno., 39.
Sleigh, Sam., 51.
Smallbones, Jno., 40.
Smith, (—), 45.
........., Ant., 60.
........., Ben., 54.
........., Geo., 29.
........., Hugh, 60.
........., Jno., 60.
........., Sam., 54.
........., Thos., 39.
Sotheby, Jno., 69.
Southby, Jno. *See supra*.
Spence, (—), 18.
Spicer, Giles, 2.
Spottiswood, Alex., 1, 45.
Stalker, Jas., 13.
Stapleton, Abr., 63.
Stapylton, Bryan, 51.
Stearne, Robt., 54. *See* Sterne.
Stedman, Chas., 69.
Stephens, Giles, 45.
Stephenson, Geo., 2, 16 *bis*.
Sterne, Robt., 54.
Stewart, (—), 67.
........., Hen., 66.
........., Jas. (Rl. Scots Greys), 24.
........., Jas. (Rl. Regt. of Foot), 33.
........., Jno. (Rl. Scots Greys), 24.
........., Jno. (Rl. Scots Fusiliers), 57
........., Peter, 33.
Stevenson, Robt., 67.
Stirrop, Thos., 13.
Stone, Wm., 20.
Straiton, Alex., 57.
........., David, 57.
........., Jas., 36.
........., Robt. (Rl. Regt. of Foot), 33.
........., Robt. (Rl. Scots Fusiliers), 57.
Stroud, Jos., 54.
Sutherland, Jas., 45.
Sutton, Ric., 42.

T

Tancred, Jas., 48, 72.
Tatton, Wm., 63.
Taylor, Robt., 54.
Teale, Isaac, 12.
Temple, Edwin, 48.
Têtefolle, Claude, 22.
Thomas, Tim., 63.
Thomson, Clifton, 20 *bis*, 72.

Tichborne, Ben., 63, 72.
Timpson, Thos., 69.
Trevelyan, Walt., 57.
Tripp, Robt., 54.
Tunbridge, Wm. Henry de Nassau, Lord, 2.

U

Usher, Jno., 13.

V

Vandergracht, Jno., 57, 72.
Vauclin, (—), 54.
Ventris, Peyton, 51.
Vernal, Wm., 36.
Vickeridge, Fry, 51.
Villebonne, Jno., 48.

W

Walker, (—), 42.
........., Thos., 48.
Wall, Garret, 57.
Walley, Jno., 63.
Walsh, Edw., 54.
........., Hen., 54.
........., Ralph, 69.
Ward, Ric., 20.
Warren, Wm., 63.
Watkins, Geo., 2, 63.
........., Hen., 2.
Watson, Jonas, 8.
Wauchope, J——, 33.
Watts, Mat., 27.
Webb, Jno. Richmond, 1, 42.
Weddall, Wm., 54.
Weekes, Jno., 45, 72.
Weems, (—). *See* Wemyss.

Weir, Wm., 34.
Weldon, Robt., 54.
Wells, Dr., 22.
........., Walter, 20.
Wemyss, (—), 66.
West, Jno., 29.
........., Wm., 29.
Whaley, Edw., 16.
Whitaker, Hen., 13.
White, Alex., 33.
........., Jas., 33.
........., Lt.-Col. Jno., 33, 72.
........., Surgeon's Mate Jno., 46.
........., Thos., 39.
Whitehall, Jno., 63.
Whitfield, Jno., 51, 72.
Whitney, Hen., 2, 42 *bis*.
........., Thos., 2, 48.
Williams, Wm., 57.
Williamson, Adam, 69.
Wilson, Cornet Arch., 24.
........., Lieut. Arch., 66.
........., Jno., 66.
........., Robt., 2, 13.
........., Thos., 12.
Windham, Wm., 20.
Windsor, And., 29.
Wingfield, Hen., 48.
Wiseman, Chas., 13.
Withers, Hen., 1, 29.
Wood, Cornelius, 1, 16.
........., Paul, 69.
Wynue, Owen, 27.

Y

Young, Jno., 60.
........., Thos., 34, 72.

Z

Zulestein, Maurice, 29.

www.ingramcontent.com/pod-product-compliance
Ingram Content Group UK Ltd.
Pitfield, Milton Keynes, MK11 3LW, UK
UKHW042006230426
12048UKWH00009B/595